Ian MacDonald and Brian Russell

ESSENTIALS

GCSE Design & Technology
Product Design
Revision Guide

Contents

Contents

Materials (Cont.)

Processing Materials

History of Product Design

Design Movements

Product design has always been **influenced** by...
- the discovery of new materials
- iconic products
- manufacturing and technological developments
- fashions, trends and the latest thinking.

These influences lead to the emergence of new, distinct styles at certain times in history. These are called **design movements**.

You should have a basic knowledge of the major design movements, so that you can recognise their influences in new and existing designs.

Influences of Nature

The **Arts and Crafts movement** (1890s) was founded by William Morris:
- It promoted quality craftsmanship.
- It was inspired by natural patterns and forms.
- It used high-quality materials, which were only affordable by the wealthy.

Art Nouveau developed in Europe from 1890–1914:
- It was based on natural, organic lines.
- It included designers like Charles Rennie Mackintosh and Louis Comfort Tiffany.

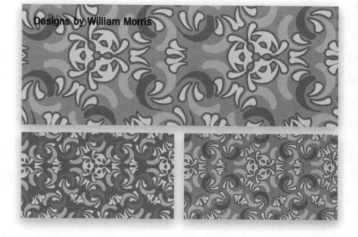
Designs by William Morris

Influences of Industry

The **Modernist** movement was influenced by industrial designs and made use of geometric shapes.

The **Bauhaus** movement (1919–1933) was a German school of art and design:
- It produced the first design for mass production.
- It was the origin of many 'design classics'.

Art Deco (1920s–1930s) began with an exhibition of products in Paris in 1925:
- It typically involved the use of geometric shapes.
- It was influenced by artefacts in Tutankhamen's recently opened tomb.
- It included the ceramicist Claris Cliff.
- It was regarded as a 'glamorous' period.

De Stijl (The Style, mid-1920s) started in Holland:
- It featured extreme geometric design, e.g. rectangles and primary colours.

- It inspired completely new designs in furniture and architecture.
- It included the painter, Piet Mondrian, and designer Gerrit Rietveld (red and blue chair design classic).

Art Deco

War, Post-war and the 1960s

The **Streamlined Age** was about speed and movement. New materials and production methods allowed designs to be manufactured cheaply. There were three main influences:

- The rapid growth in transport design.
- The interest in science.
- The race to put the first man on the moon.

In the **1960s** there was huge consumer growth as consumers craved new ideas:

- The 'Mods' represented the first separate teenage consumer market.
- Designers included Mary Quant (designer of the mini skirt) and Alec Issigonis (Morris Mini).

Morris Mini

1970–Present Day

By the 1980s the **designer name** or brand was important to consumers:

- The **designer label** spread from fashion markets to other areas of product design.
- Promotion and packaging became a key part of the complete product.

The **Memphis Group** (early 1980s) was an alternative viewpoint to minimalism:

- It was started by a group of Italian designers, led by Ettore Sottsass.
- They produced highly-decorative laminates and humorous products.
- Their post-modernism influence can be seen in many of today's products.

Blobism is a current trend characterised by a lack of straight lines and produced in a variety of ways. The development of sophisticated CAD software has allowed complex flowing forms to be designed and manufactured.

N.B. Pages 4–7 give examples of eras, trends and iconic designs. If you are sitting the OCR exam you need to know a specific list of eras, trend setters and icons – check with your teacher or on the OCR website.

Memphis Group

CAD Software

Classic Designs

Design Icons

Some products are so **innovative** and influential that they are regarded as **classic designs** or **design icons**.

A design could be considered to be iconic because…
- of the way that technology has been used
- it uses clever and innovative styling
- it simply has a 'must own' quality.

Some Classic Designs

There are many examples of classic designs, a few of which are detailed below. You need to be able to identify and discuss the influences on iconic designs.

The **Coca-Cola** bottle (1916) is a globally recognised object and has remained largely unchanged since its design in 1916, mainly due to its…
- distinctive shape
- brand name.

László and George **Bíró** designed the first ballpoint pen in 1931. In 1950, Marcel Bich purchased the Bíró patent and it became the main product of his **BIC** company. The word **biro** is used today to describe all ballpoint pens.

The **Volkswagen Beetle** (1930s) was designed by Ferdinand Porsche and was given its name by the *New York Times* due to its unusual shape. There is a clear influence from this design on the current VW Beetle.

Marcel Breuer's Wassily Chair, designed in 1925, was the first tubular-steel chair. It was apparently inspired by a bicycle frame and uses the Bauhaus principle(s) of form following function.

Philippe Starck's Juicy Salif **lemon squeezer** was very controversial, with critics saying it was extravagant and unpractical. But, it's very popular with many people.

Harry Beck's diagrammatic map of the **London Underground** is a graphical design which spreads out the centre of the city and compresses the outskirts. It doesn't represent the actual geographical position of places, but it's easy to understand and the format has been copied all over the world.

Bíró

Volkswagen Beetle

Philippe Starck's Juicy Salif Lemon Squeezer

Retro Styling

Retro styling has become very popular. **Retro designs** aren't old-fashioned products. They are based on old styles, but made to the latest standards using the latest technologies. For example, some modern radios are modelled on Lawrence Griffin's 1950s design.

Retro design is commonly seen…

- where there is a strong surface decoration, e.g. wallpaper, fabrics and ceramics
- in electrical appliances, e.g. DeLonghi toaster
- in transport design, e.g. Chrysler PT Cruiser
- in fashion, e.g. in 1965 Yves St Laurent designed a dress based on Piet Mondrian's work about 40 years earlier.

Retro Radio

Chrysler PT Cruiser

DeLonghi Toaster

A Retro Diner

Quick Test

1. Give two factors that influence the design of products.
2. What was the main influence of the Modernist movement?
3. Give one example of a retro-styled design.
4. What is Blobism?
5. Name two iconic designs.

KEY WORDS

Make sure you understand these words before moving on!

- Influence
- Design movements
- Arts and Crafts movement
- Art Nouveau
- Modernism
- Bauhaus
- Art Deco
- De Stijl
- Designer name
- Designer label
- Memphis Group
- Blobism
- Innovation
- Classic design
- Design icon
- Retro design

Market Pull and Technological Push

New Products

There are many reasons why a new product is developed. The two main terms that you need to understand are...

- **market pull**
- **technological push**.

A push / pull effect creates demands that are met by the development of products.

Market Pull

The market place creates **consumer demand**. Consumers see a product that they want to buy. This creates a demand for the product and can often lead to development and expansion of that product.

Manufacturers can help to create consumer demand, for example with the Sony Walkman in the late 1970s. The technology had been around for some time, but consumer demand suddenly increased when Sony developed a product for people to listen to music whilst on the move.

Millions of personal stereos in many different styling versions have been sold and many other products have now developed from this product, for example portable CD players and MP3 players.

Technological Push

Some new products are developed due to the technological advance of...

- new materials
- production methods.

Scientists develop a new material, and an imaginative designer then thinks of a use for the material in a commercial application.

Examples:

1. **Microwave** ovens were developed from Second World War RADAR technology.

2. A chemist, Roy J. Plunkett, discovered polytetrafluoroethylene (PTFE) resin while researching refrigerants at DuPont. This new material (now known as **Teflon**) is very heat-tolerant and stick-resistant. Teflon coating has been used on...

- space satellites
- non-stick pans.

Teflon-coated Griddle Pan

Quality Control Guidelines

Products can **evolve** as manufacturers aim to **constantly improve** their products. This is part of **Total Quality Management** (TQM).

Recognised standards, for example, BS EN ISO 9000:2005 are guidelines by which companies are assessed. Customers then know that a product made to these standards will conform to specific quality and safety checks.

Companies are **continually assessed**, so they need to spend time looking at…
- the way they work
- how they can improve their products or manufacturing methods.

Everyone in a company will be involved in this process, so there are **standard controls** that help to make sure that everything is done in an orderly and controlled way:

- Every part of a product is specified and documented.
- There are set procedures to follow if anyone thinks there is a problem with a product.
- Changes need to be authorised by a senior person.

When dealing with a complicated product, e.g. a car, the process can become very complex. For example, the workforce may be in different parts of a country, or even in different countries.

Many sources are included in the continuous improvement process. The **manufacturing specification** is continually updated and agreed with the client. Manufacturers create **quality circles** – groups of workers who feedback information to ensure the quality of the product is continually improving.

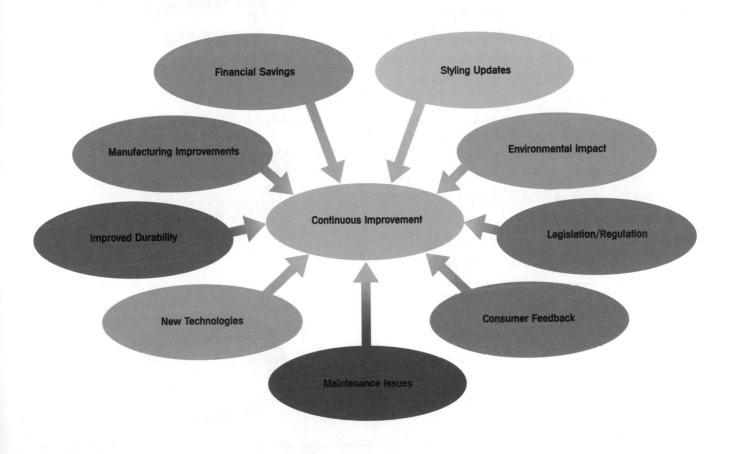

Product Evolution

Why Products Evolve

Products also develop over time due to...
- developments in new materials, e.g. smart materials
- changes in manufacturing methods, e.g. automated production processes
- new technologies, e.g. **micro-electronics**
- **social changes**, e.g. women going out to work
- changing fashions, e.g. seasonal colours in textile products.

Example: The Iron

The iron has evolved dramatically since the 1900s.

At the beginning of the 20th Century, irons had several basic features: • Manufactured locally using cast iron. • Had a hollow, wrought iron handle that remained cool. • Heated on a coal or wood-burning stove. • Mainly used to iron cotton and linen. • A damp cloth was used if a fabric was too dry.	
As homes became linked to an **energy supply**, coal gas was used for lighting and heating: • Gas was used to heat up the soleplate. • A turned wooden handle was used for its insulating properties. • Enamelled coatings were used to improve the appearance.	
The introduction of **electricity** into homes led to the development of a wide range of electrical products: • An electrical element was used to heat the sole-plate (but could only be controlled by turning off the electric supply). • Was mainly used to iron cotton and linen. • Made from lots of different components.	
Ceramics were developed and were used for their insulating properties: • The ceramic body could cover the electrical element and allow the designer to add colour. • **Bakelite** plastic was commonly used by the 1940s and allowed product styling to really develop.	

Example: The Iron (Cont.)

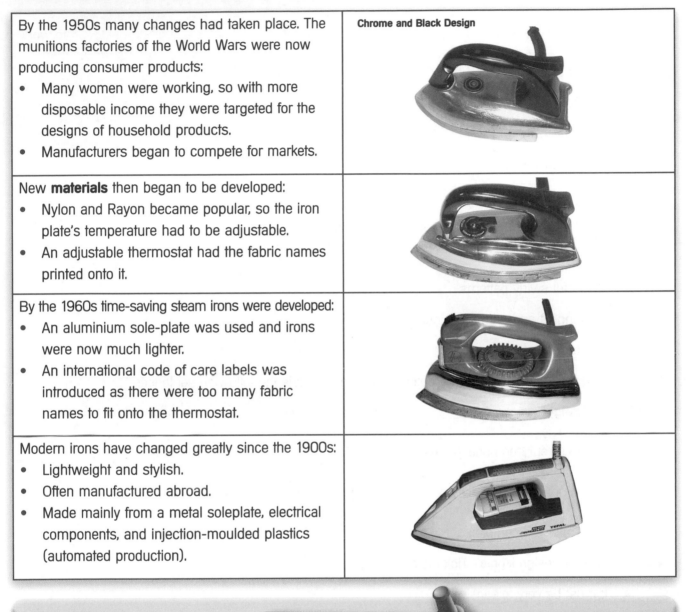

By the 1950s many changes had taken place. The munitions factories of the World Wars were now producing consumer products: • Many women were working, so with more disposable income they were targeted for the designs of household products. • Manufacturers began to compete for markets.	**Chrome and Black Design**
New **materials** then began to be developed: • Nylon and Rayon became popular, so the iron plate's temperature had to be adjustable. • An adjustable thermostat had the fabric names printed onto it.	
By the 1960s time-saving steam irons were developed: • An aluminium sole-plate was used and irons were now much lighter. • An international code of care labels was introduced as there were too many fabric names to fit onto the thermostat.	
Modern irons have changed greatly since the 1900s: • Lightweight and stylish. • Often manufactured abroad. • Made mainly from a metal soleplate, electrical components, and injection-moulded plastics (automated production).	

Quick Test

1. Give the two main reasons for the development of a new product.
2. Why would a company use recognised standards on products?
3. Give three reasons why a product might evolve over time.
4. Give two developments / changes that led to the evolution of the iron.

KEY WORDS

Make sure you understand these words before moving on!

- Market pull
- Technological push
- Consumer demand
- Microwaves
- Continuous improvement
- Total quality management
- Continuous assessment
- Standard controls
- Manufacturing specification
- Quality circles
- Micro-electronics
- Social change
- Bakelite

Practice Questions

1 Give two factors that have historically influenced product design.

   a) _____

   b) _____

2 What was Art Deco influenced by? Tick the correct option.

   A Nature   ☐

   B Animals   ☐

   C Wave movement   ☐

   D Industry   ☐

3 What kind of styles was De Stijl famous for? Tick the correct option.

   A Black and white prints   ☐

   B Colourful swirly patterns   ☐

   C Rectangles and primary colours   ☐

   D Abstract paintings   ☐

4 Choose the correct words from the options given to complete the following sentences.

CAD   **straight**   **CAM**   **flowing**   **curved**

Blobism is a current trend characterised by a lack of _____ lines.

Blobjects is produced in a variety of ways, but the development of sophisticated _____

software has allowed complex _____ forms to be designed and manufactured.

5 What makes a design iconic? Tick the correct option.

   A It must be very expensive   ☐

   B It must be colourful   ☐

   C It must be traditional   ☐

   D It must be innovative   ☐

6 Circle the correct options in the following sentences.

A Volkswagen **Beetle / Polo** is an iconic design. The design might have changed slightly over the years but its **shape / size** is recognisable all over the world.

7 In what products can retro styling often be seen? Tick the **two** correct options.

A On planes ☐

B On cars ☐

C In fashion ☐

D In food ☐

8 Name one recognised standard that provides guidelines by which companies are assessed.

....

9 What is a **quality circle**?

....

....

10 Briefly explain how market pull can create the development of a new product.

....

....

....

11 Match changes **A, B, C** and **D** with the results **1–4** in the table. Enter the appropriate number in the boxes provided.

	Results
1	Women going out to work
2	Automated production processes
3	Smart materials
4	Seasonal colours in textile products

A Developments in new materials ☐

B Changing fashions ☐

C Changes in manufacturing methods ☐

D Social changes ☐

Sustainability Issues

Effect on the Environment

Any action that we take has an impact on the environment. **Sustainability** is about meeting the needs and demands of society without depleting resources or harming natural cycles for future generations.

All raw materials are taken from the planet and waste products remain with us in some form:

- **Renewable materials** are grown from plants or animals.
- **Non-renewable materials** are taken from oil, ores and minerals, and can't be replaced (they are **finite**).

You need to ensure that you…

- use resources carefully
- avoid using solutions that create a problem for someone else
- try to improve your environment, don't damage it.

In order to minimise the environmental impact of using raw materials, designers should consider the 6 Rs:

- **Reduce** the amount of material used in manufacture.
- **Recycle** the materials already used.
- **Re-use** design for disassembly and recover materials from 'end of life' products.
- **Repair** products that have broken rather than replacing them.
- **Refuse** to accept unethical or wasteful designs.
- **Re-think** our attitude to environmental impact.

Recycling / Disposing of Products

It's very important that we all dispose of products carefully and responsibly.

Products and packaging have symbols on them to show…

- if they can be recycled
- the percentage of recyclable material used
- the materials they are made from, e.g. the type of plastic polymer used
- if a fee has been paid to recover packaging (the Green Dot symbol used in many European countries)
- materials that can be sorted and separated for recycling
- products that can't be disposed of in normal household bins, e.g. electrical products and batteries.

Recycle Now Icon

Percentage of Recycled Material

x%

Green Dot Symbol

Do Not Dispose of Items in General Rubbish Bins

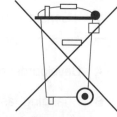

Identifies the Type of Plastic

1 PETE — Polyethylene Terepthalate

6 PS — Polystyrene

Re-using Materials

Products can also be **re-used**. This reduces the amount of processing needed, so it's cheaper and more environmentally friendly.

Standardising parts means that materials can be re-used easily.

Examples of re-using materials include...
- refilling plastic or glass containers
- re-using car parts
- re-using clothing / shoes.

Carbon Footprint and Product Miles

A **carbon footprint** is the amount of carbon produced by any human activity and its effects on the environment. It's measured in units of **carbon dioxide**.

So, every activity you undertake and every product you use can be measured in terms of the...
- amount of energy used at every stage
- the carbon emissions produced.

Product miles are the number of miles a product travels in its lifetime. For example, a typical product might travel as follows: Source material to the primary processor ⟶ Material to the factory ⟶ Product to the distributor ⟶ Distributor to the retail outlet ⟶ Retail outlet to the user's home ⟶ From home to recycling or tip.

You should consider...
- what effect these product miles have on the environment
- how much energy is consumed through transporting materials, components and products.

Product Life Cycles

The diagram illustrates some of the options available when considering product **life cycles**.

Approximately 90% of oil is burned as heating and transport fuel.

About 7% of oil is used to manufacture plastics.

Some plastics are dumped in landfill sites.

Some plastics are burned, which causes toxic fumes to be released into the atmosphere.

Many plastics can be recycled. They need to be collected and sorted into their different types.

The pellets can be mixed with virgin plastic and moulded into new products.

The recycled plastics are melted and extruded into pellets.

Once sorted, the plastics can be granulated and cleaned to remove any impurities.

Packaging

Packaging

Most products have some form of **packaging** that is used for different reasons:

- **Protection** – needed during transit and is often a box with a protective inner.
- **Information** – to give users knowledge about the product, e.g. technical information and symbols.
- **Display** – so the product can be clearly seen.
- **Transportation** – e.g. wooden pallets make bulk transportation easier.
- **Containing** – to keep any loose materials or components together.
- **Preservation** – against the weather, temperature, bacteria, etc.

Packaging Symbols

Packaging symbols inform consumers about hazards, storage and handling, maintenance, disposal and design protection. For example…

- fragile contents, handle with care
- do not allow packaging to get wet
- flammable, toxic or corrosive contents
- environmental symbols, e.g. recycling symbols
- maintenance symbols, e.g. on clothes.

Bar codes represent data in a machine-readable form. The scanned data is sent to a computer system where it's recorded and processed. Bar codes are used for…

- stock control
- pricing
- to eliminate human error
- to check on consumer buying trends
- recording points, e.g. on customer loyalty cards.

Fragile   Keep Contents Dry

Flammable   Corrosive

Barcode

9 781903 068434

Food Labelling

Food **labelling** is covered by **legislation** and manufacturers must follow strict guidelines.

Legal requirements control what must be written and included on food labels:

- **Name** of product – by law this can't be misleading, e.g. 'Strawberry yoghurt' must **contain** strawberries, but 'Strawberry flavoured yoghurt' just needs to **taste** of strawberries.
- List of **ingredients** – all the ingredients must be listed in decreasing order of weight, including additives and preservatives. This allows you to compare products or avoid foods you can't / don't want to eat.
- Best before and use by **dates** – products can't be sold beyond these, and a product should be thrown away once the **use by** date has passed.
- **Storage** instructions – particularly important after a food product has been opened.
- **Nutritional** information – provided so you can compare products.
- **Contact** details of the maker, packer or seller.

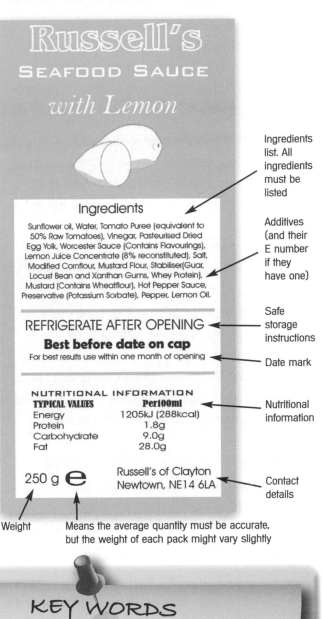

Russell's SEAFOOD SAUCE with Lemon

Ingredients — Ingredients list. All ingredients must be listed

Sunflower oil, Water, Tomato Puree (equivalent to 50% Raw Tomatoes), Vinegar, Pasteurised Dried Egg Yolk, Worcester Sauce (Contains Flavourings), Lemon Juice Concentrate (8% reconstituted), Salt, Modified Cornflour, Mustard Flour, Stabiliser(Guar, Locust Bean and Xanthan Gums, Whey Protein), Mustard (Contains Wheatflour), Hot Pepper Sauce, Preservative (Potassium Sorbate), Pepper, Lemon Oil. — Additives (and their E number if they have one)

REFRIGERATE AFTER OPENING — Safe storage instructions

Best before date on cap
For best results use within one month of opening — Date mark

NUTRITIONAL INFORMATION — Nutritional information

TYPICAL VALUES	Per100ml
Energy	1205kJ (288kcal)
Protein	1.8g
Carbohydrate	9.0g
Fat	28.0g

250 g ℮   Russell's of Clayton Newtown, NE14 6LA — Contact details

Weight

Means the average quantity must be accurate, but the weight of each pack might vary slightly

Quick Test

1. What is sustainability?
2. What does a Green Dot symbol mean on a piece of plastic packaging?
3. Give two examples of products that could be re-used.
4. What is a **carbon footprint**?
5. Give six reasons why a product might be packaged.

Flat Pack Furniture

Flat Pack Furniture

Many products are manufactured as **flat pack furniture**, so they can be assembled at home by the consumer. This saves on storage and transportation costs so the end product is cheaper for the consumers.

There are several key issues for flat packed furniture:

- The material used for the main construction must be cheap and consistent in quality. It's often pre-finished, e.g. a plastic edge might be glued on.
- All of the parts are drilled ready for assembly.
- Some **sub-assemblies** have been produced to ensure accuracy of assembly.
- It must be easy to put together as it might be assembled by someone without prior knowledge or skills.
- Packaging, storage and transportation must be considered carefully, e.g. small / medium sized products can often be lifted and carried by one person.
- Quality assurance is essential. Any single component must be accurate enough to be assembled without further working.
- Computer-aided machinery can be used to ensure accuracy and to reduce wastage.

Packaging

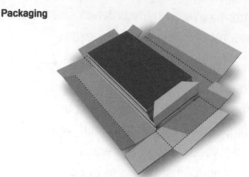

Using KD Fittings and Dowels

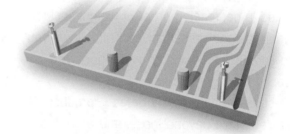

Finished Product

Assembly and Instruction Booklets

Assembly and instruction booklets need to be well thought out. They may need to be very detailed, depending on the product, e.g. electrical goods.

These booklets...

- tell the consumer how to assemble the product
- tell the consumer how to use the product
- need to be easy to understand regardless of the country of manufacture (graphics can be used to overcome language barriers).

Using Graphics in an Instruction Booklet

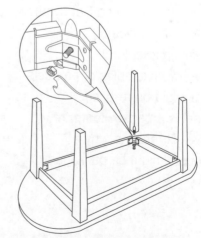

Product Maintenance

Many products have a life expectancy based on some degree of **maintenance**:

- Simple products, e.g. personal stereos, need to have the batteries changed regularly.
- Complex products, e.g. cars, have very detailed maintenance schedules. Records are kept so that the manufacturer's warranty is valid.

Food products often have a lifespan written into their specification and have specific storage requirements, e.g. 'Use by' or 'Best before' dates. A safety margin is normally built into the specification.

Many products are developed simply to meet these maintenance requirements. Other products require regular maintenance to keep them in good working condition.

Symbols

Clothing manufacturers have agreed an international code to help with product maintenance. Clothing care symbols include the following:

- Ironing temperatures (the same simple dot code is found on irons).
- Tumble drying.
- Fabric material care labels. Wool, silk, cotton and linen have these labels. Fabrics like Lycra or Tactel usually carry their own trademark.
- Washing symbols – a complex mixture of images and bars that tell the consumer what water temperature or washing machine cycle to use.

N.B. Any symbol with a cross through it means that you can't do that activity.

Other symbols **inform** the consumer about the maintenance and storage of products. For example...

- product is suitable for freezing
- keep away from magnetic fields
- keep away from naked flames
- low battery
- store this way up
- be careful when lifting.

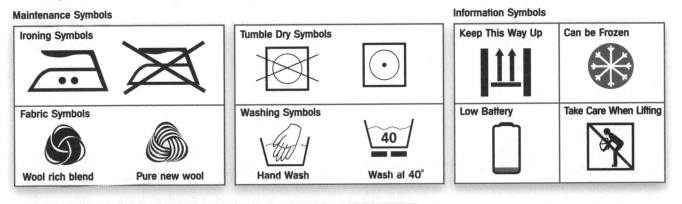

Maintenance Symbols

Ironing Symbols

Fabric Symbols — Wool rich blend — Pure new wool

Tumble Dry Symbols

Washing Symbols — Hand Wash — Wash at 40°

Information Symbols

Keep This Way Up — Can be Frozen

Low Battery — Take Care When Lifting

Designed Obsolescence & Standard Components

Designed obsolescence or **planned obsolescence** is where a product has been designed to be thrown away after a certain period of time, e.g. disposal razors and cameras. These products maybe convenient to use, but they often use up the same amounts of raw materials and energy as more long-lasting products, i.e. they aren't environmentally friendly.

Using **standard components** makes it easier to maintain products. For example...

- using plain white buttons on shirts makes replacement easy
- standardising screw threads means products can be repaired easily.

Human Factors

Human Factors

Most products are designed for humans, so when designing a product you need to consider **human factors**, for example…
- physiological factors
- psychological factors
- sociological factors.

If you're designing entirely for animals then a similar investigation might be needed, but you may find that the information is harder to find.

Stereotypes

Everyone is unique (different), but people are often **stereotyped** (classed in groups). These stereotypes can be useful to designers, manufacturers and especially retailers.

It's common practice to aim a product at a particular **target market** or **target user**.

Inclusive and Exclusive Design

An **ideal product** is one that can be used by everyone. This is known as **inclusive design** and, although it's an impossible aim, designers should design products that are suitable for as many people as possible.

Some products have to be designed to take into account the **specific** needs of people, e.g. the very young or the elderly. Examples of **exclusive design** are car seats for babies and wheelchairs for disabled people.

Quick Test

1. Give one instruction method that can be used in assembly booklets so they would be understood by people of different nationalities.
2. Sketch the symbol that shows that clothing can be tumble dried.
3. Sketch the symbol that shows that a product can be frozen.
4. What is inclusive design?
5. Why is exclusive design easier to achieve than inclusive design?

KEY WORDS
Make sure you understand these words before moving on!
- Sub-assembly
- Maintenance
- Planned obsolescence
- Standard components
- Human factors
- Stereotypes
- Target market
- Inclusive design
- Exclusive design

Physiological Factors

Physiological factors are concerned with the **physical** limitations of people.

In general we all move our bodies in similar ways and we have similar hand / eye co-ordination. But, we do vary greatly in…

- size
- strength
- levels of stamina.

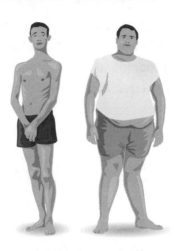

Anthropometrics

Anthropometrics is the study of the human body and the movement of each part of the body. When designing a product you must consider the person or people you are designing for (e.g. adults and children vary greatly in size).

Anthropometric data is **measurements** that have been taken from millions of people of all shapes and sizes and put together in charts.

With so many measurements it can be difficult to know which ones to choose when designing a product. Designers try to work from the 5th to the 95th percentile, which means that 90% of the population are catered for.

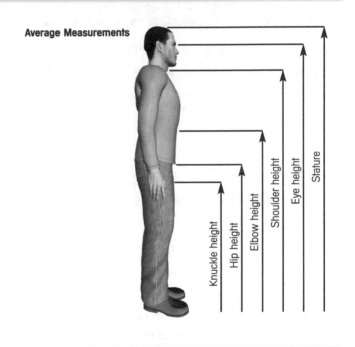

Average Measurements

Knuckle height · Hip height · Elbow height · Shoulder height · Eye height · Stature

Ergonomics

Ergonomics is the study of efficiency of people in their working environment. It often deals with the application of anthropometric data.

Designers always look at ergonomics with a view to making things easier for people to use. They consider a list of categories when designing a new product, including factors such as comfort and safety.

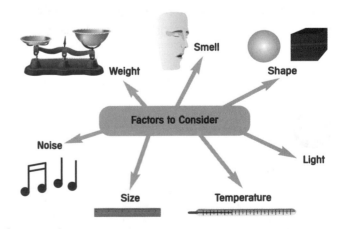

Weight · Smell · Shape · Noise · Factors to Consider · Light · Size · Temperature

Human Factors

Working Triangles

Ergonomics is often concerned with the efficient organisation and management of work space. The term **working triangle** is used to describe the range of movement needed for a particular task.

Working triangles are often used when…
- planning kitchens
- designing driving positions in cars, sometimes known as the **reach envelope** (the driver is in a fixed position so every control needs to be comfortably within reach).

Adjustment

Products often need to **adjustable** because people vary so much in size, weight, etc. An adjustable product is suitable for a wide range of users, for example…

- office chairs
- car seats
- bicycles.

Psychological Factors

Psychological factors are concerned with how the brain works. We have five **senses** that constantly feed messages back to the brain:
- Touch
- Taste

- Smell
- Sound
- Sight

When they design a product, designers need to understand how people think and react to these senses.

Touch, Taste and Smell

Comfort and **touch** are important factors when looking at products. Products can be designed to…
- provide a textured surface
- be warm or cool to the touch
- work with just the sense of touch, e.g. game consoles and computer mice.

Temperature is a factor with many products. For example, designers need to consider how hot the body of a toaster could be before it would become too hot to touch.

Taste is a major factor in many products and some products have been designed to appeal to our sense of taste, for example…
- toothpaste
- lip gloss.

Smell is an important factor when developing food and other everyday products. Smell has a big influence on our sense of taste. Cosmetics and household fragrances are two product areas where smell is important. For example…
- the smell of lemon often suggests cleanliness
- the smell of pine suggests fresh air.

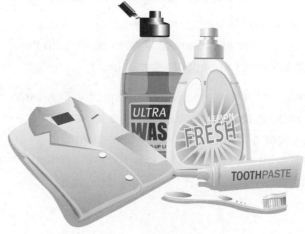

Sound and Sight

Loud noises can be a nuisance but, because we normally react to noise, **sound** is used as a warning in many products. Products that rely on our sense of hearing include…

- fire alarms
- car horns
- alarm clocks.

The volume and range of noise have to be considered though. If the noise is too loud it could be a danger.

Sight is one of our most sophisticated senses. Designers need to consider how people see and respond to visual information, e.g. digital or analogue displays, symbols and signage.

Designers can design 'attractive' products using different colours and shapes. Colour can…

- create the feeling of warmth or coolness
- alert us to danger
- suggest issues such as cleanliness, femininity and masculinity.

Sociological Factors

Sociological factors are concerned with people living and working together. These issues are important in transport design and architecture, for example looking at…

- how much 'personal space' people need on a bus
- the size of rooms in buildings.

Disability

We are all 'disabled' at some time in our lives, for example…

- we rely on our parents to transport us when we are very young
- many of us will experience mobility problems as we get older.

But, for some people, disability is a permanent feature of their lives. Designers must be fully aware of the needs of all areas of disability in order to make their products more **inclusive**. This is particularly important for public spaces and services, for example phone booths, public buildings and public transport.

Human Factors

Access

Designers need to consider how easy or difficult it is to **access** certain products:

- Providing lifts in buildings, disabled parking bays and Braille signage are simple solutions to include a wider range of users.
- Products can be made easier to use if they have simple controls and don't rely on language skills.

- Some products may be difficult to open, especially if the user has limited strength.
- Many products are packaged specifically to restrict access to certain groups, e.g. child-proof locks, but these can cause problems for other users.

Safety

Safety is a major issue for product designers and is relevant in all the areas of human factors. For example, you might need to consider…

- how large a component needs to be so that it can't be swallowed
- how wide the bars on a cot should be in order to prevent babies getting their heads stuck
- how hot the outside of a kettle gets.

Dietary Needs

Food products need to take into account the different **dietary** needs between people. There are many reasons for the differences in people's eating habits:

- People have different likes and dislikes.
- The daily intake of food that people need varies, e.g. an athlete needs a higher intake than an office worker.

- Growing children have different food needs from those of the elderly.
- Some people have allergies to foods such as gluten or nuts.
- People who are vegetarians will have different dietary needs from those people who eat meat and vegetables.

Quick Test

1. What percentage of measurements would you use to cover the largest section of the population?
2. What is the most efficient working space known as?
3. What is the study of human measurement called?
4. What are sociological factors concerned with?

KEY WORDS

Make sure you understand these words before moving on!

- Physiological
- Anthropometrics
- Ergonomics
- Working triangle
- Adjustable
- Psychological
- Touch
- Taste
- Smell
- Sound
- Sight
- Sociological
- Diet

Regulations

When designing products you should be aware that there is a wide range of **regulations** and **legislation** aimed at protecting the consumer.

- Some regulatory bodies are set up by **manufacturing groups** to ensure that all their members follow their voluntary codes of practice. They provide guidance to designers and manufacturers.
- Some regulations are governed by **Acts of Parliament**.

Legislation

You don't need to know the details of each regulation, but you should be aware that different regulatory bodies govern certain areas. For example:

- The **Trade Descriptions Act** makes it illegal to make false claims about a product.
- The **Weights and Measures Act** makes it illegal to sell products that are underweight or short-measured.
- The **Consumer Safety Act** allows the Government to ban the sale of dangerous products.
- The **Consumer Protection Act** prevents the sale of harmful or defective products.

- The **Sale of Goods Act** states that products must be fit for their purpose.
- The **Food Safety Regulations** and the **Food Safety Act** provides guidance on food hygiene management.
- The **Food Labelling Regulations** states that certain information must be included on labels.

When labelling a product or packaging you have designed, you should think about...

- including a description of how it might be used
- who the user might be
- any technical information that might need to be included.

Standards and the Consumers' Association

Products and components are checked using tests devised by the **British Standards Institution** (BSI). A **standard** is an agreed specification for a product or service. The Kitemark scheme is an independent and ongoing assessment that the product conforms to the relevant standard. BSI standards are very precise specifications and manufacturers who meet these standards are awarded a **Kitemark**:

- The **Kitemark** is a test against nationally recognised standards.
- The **Conformité Européenne** 'CE' symbol tells you that the product meets the minimum requirements from the EU directive to be allowed to be put on sale.

The **Consumers' Association** publishes the *Which?* magazine. In each edition, products are tested against other similar products and graded against criteria such as 'value for money'. Many libraries carry *Which?* reports.

Branding

Brand Creation

You need to understand the importance of **branding** and **advertising** on different target markets and how you could brand your own products.

Branding is about promoting **your** strengths, i.e. what **your** business is good at or what **you** believe in, for example...

- offering the latest technology
- giving high-quality customer care and technical back-up
- giving best value for money in the marketplace.

Also known as **brand values**, these are promises that a business makes to its customers. It's important to keep the brand simple by focusing on a small number of key brand values.

Maintaining & Communicating the Brand

Businesses need to **maintain** their brand by...

- focusing on what the business achieves for its customers and continually looking for ways to improve
- being honest (not making claims that they can't deliver)
- being consistent (just one failure can damage the brand)
- paying attention to customers' needs, but still controlling the brand message.

Most businesses **communicate** their brand by creating a **logo** which they will then use on advertisements, catalogues, brochures and stationery. These logos will often be important to image-conscious consumers.

As consumers, we are offered a wide choice of branded products and it can be difficult to make the right decisions about what we purchase:

- Do we purchase products because of our **brand loyalty**?
- Do these brands reassure you of the quality you expect or do they suggest exploitation of workers, environmental concerns or other moral issues?

Protecting the Brand

Designers' ideas can be protected by law to stop anyone copying them. This is called **intellectual property**. For example, logos are often protected under intellectual property legislation and businesses defend the use of them. This is sometimes referred to as **design protection**.

- **Copyright** is commonly used for publications and building plans.
- **Registered designs** (sometimes with a registration number) offer proof of ownership and are used to protect the form or style of a product or logo.
- **Trademarks** are also registered and become a major part of the brand as they protect names, symbols and logos.
- **Patents** are used to protect inventions, new technologies or new processes. The patent could be worldwide or restricted to certain countries, e.g. James Dyson holds numerous patents for his vacuum cleaners.

License Agreement

Many ideas are allowed to be used by others through a **license agreement**. This is a contract between the owner and a manufacturer and will be linked to payments.

For example, Disney allow products to be manufactured that use their cartoon characters, but they have strict license agreements that protect the image and maintain the quality associated with Disney products. This is an essential part of maintaining their brand.

You can use existing logos and cartoon characters when designing products, but you will need to explain the licensing issues that you have to follow before you can consider going into commercial production.

Fairtrade Brand

The **Fairtrade** mark is an independent consumer label that appears on products as an independent guarantee that disadvantaged producers in the developing world are getting a better deal. These producers receive…

- a minimum price that covers the cost of sustainable production
- an extra premium that's invested in social or economic development projects.

Quick Test

1 In which two ways are regulatory bodies governed?

2 What is a Kitemark?

3 What are **brand values**?

4 By what branch of law are logos protected?

5 What does the Fairtrade mark mean for the producers?

KEY WORDS

Make sure you understand these words before moving on!

- Regulation
- Legislation
- Standard
- Branding
- Advertising
- Brand values
- Logo
- Intellectual property
- Copyright
- Registered designs
- Trademarks
- Patents
- License agreement
- Fairtrade

Practice Questions

1 Why are non-renewable materials finite? Tick the correct option.

  A They will eventually run out and can't be replaced ◯

  B They will eventually run out but we can replace them ◯

  C We are constantly renewing the resources ◯

  D The resources will never run out ◯

2 Which of the following statements describe examples of re-using materials? Tick the **three** correct options.

  A Shredding cloth to make into paper ◯

  B Going to a scrap yard for car parts ◯

  C Going to a charity shop for second-hand clothing ◯

  D Refilling plastic or glass containers ◯

3 What do the following symbols mean?

a) ....

b) ....

4 What is a carbon footprint? Tick the correct option.

  A The amount of carbon dioxide used in a process ◯

  B The amount of carbon dioxide produced by any human activity ◯

  C All the greenhouse gases that are produced in a year ◯

  D The amount of carbon produced by mining coal ◯

5 Briefly explain **planned obsolescence**.

....

....

6 What do the following symbols mean?

a)  ....

b)  ....

7 What is exclusive design? Tick the correct option.

A A design that aims to be suitable for everybody ⬭

B A design that uses a specific type of material ⬭

C A design that is aimed at a specific group ⬭

D A retro design ⬭

8 Circle the correct options in the following sentences.

a) Sociological factors are concerned with **how the brain works / the physical limitations of people / how people work and live together**.

b) Psychological factors are concerned with **how the brain works / the physical limitations of people / how people work and live together**.

c) Physiological factors are concerned with **how the brain works / the physical limitations of people / how people work and live together**.

9 What is ergonomics the study of?

....

....

10 What are patents used to protect? Tick the correct option.

A Logos ⬭

B The discovery of new materials ⬭

C Mass production of a product ⬭

D New inventions ⬭

Paper and Board

Paper

Paper is a web-like material made from very fine vegetable fibres. The fibres are made of cellulose that is usually extracted from wood (though plants like hemp and flax can also be used).

The raw material is known as **wood pulp**. Chemicals are added to the wood pulp to produce the required texture and surface finish.

The following method is used to make paper:

1. Tiny chips of wood are cooked in water and chemicals to create a mushy wood pulp.
2. This pulp is then poured over a fine mesh.
3. As the water drains away the cellulose fibres (less than 1mm in length) link together when they touch.
4. The fibres are passed through a set of rollers to remove the remaining excess water. This strengthens the web of fibres.

Paper is made…

- in different sizes, e.g. A4, A3, A2
- in different weights, e.g. 100 grams per metre squared (g/m^2) is the weight of one square metre. Anything over $200g/m^2$ is classed as **board**.
- in a full range of colours by adding dyes
- with different substances by adding chemicals such as chalk.

  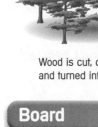

| Wood is cut, de-barked and turned into pulp | Wood pulp | Chemicals added (chalk and dye) | Mesh | Roll of paper |

Board

Board is the general term for a range of paper-based materials, for example…

- cardboard
- carton board
- mounting board
- corrugated board.

Board is made from several layers of pulp papers, so it's thicker, heavier and more rigid than paper. Very thick board is made by sticking sheets of paper or board together in a process known as **laminating**.

Paper-based board can be laminated with a wide range of other materials, e.g. aluminium foil, plaster of Paris and rigid plastic foams, to create boards with very different properties. These are often known as **composite materials**.

Types of Paper and Board

Types of Paper and Board

Description	Uses
Layout and tracing paper • Hard and translucent • Typically $50g/m^2$ • Take spirit-based marker pens well	• Used during the development stage of designing
Cartridge paper • Tough and lightly textured • Often a very light cream colour • Takes coloured pencils very well • $100–135g/m^2$	• General drawing
Cardboard • Can be laminated together to create thicker boards • From $200g/m^2$ upwards • Often made from recycled material • General purpose material	• General modelling and packaging
Solid white board • Strong, high-quality board • Made from pure bleached wood pulp • Excellent for printing onto	• Book covers • More expensive packaging
Duplex board • Made from pure wood pulp with a bleached liner on one side • Typically $250–500g/m^2$	• Food packaging (often only coated on one side)
Foil-lined board • Made by laminating aluminium foil to one side of cardboard, solid white board or duplex board • Has insulating properties • Can keep moisture in / out	• Fast-food lid containers
Corrugated board • Made up of linerboard (the flat sheet) and the medium (fluted sheet) • Available in single wall, double wall, etc • Offers strength without undue weight • Often printed in a single colour • Cheap material	• Large cartons

Timber

Timber

Timber is the general name for wood materials. There are three main types of timber.

Hardwoods come from deciduous or broad-leafed trees:
- They are generally slow growing.
- The wood is normally hard, but some is light and soft, e.g. Balsawood.
- Usually sold by the cubic metre then rough sawn to the required size.
- Can be machined into a variety of standard sections called mouldings, e.g. dowel and quadrant beading.

Softwoods come from coniferous trees that have needles instead of leaves:
- They generally grow faster than hardwoods and are usually softer to work.
- They are supplied in standard sections, rough sawn or planed smooth (planed side and edge or PSE).
- After planing the size is smaller, e.g. once planed, a 50 x 50mm section is likely to be approx. 45 x 45mm.

Manufactured boards are timber sheets made by gluing wood layers (veneers) or wood fibres together:
- Made in very large sheets of consistent quality (so used in industrial production techniques).

- Normally supplied in imperial sizes (feet and inches).
- The most common size is 8ft x 4ft (2440 x 1220mm).
- Available in a variety of thicknesses, e.g. 3mm, 6mm, 9mm, 12mm, 15mm, 18mm, etc. But, not every board is available in every thickness.
- They are examples of combined materials, especially if coated with decorative veneers or plastic laminates.

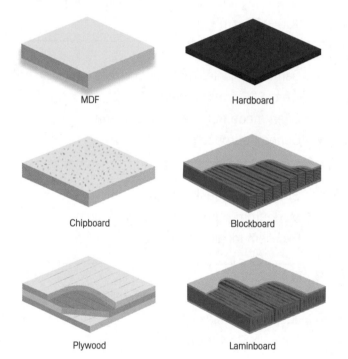

MDF   Hardboard

Chipboard   Blockboard

Plywood   Laminboard

Natural Characteristics

There are several things to consider when choosing wood for a specific purpose:
- Grain pattern – the growth ring marks visible on the surface.
- Colour – different tree species differ greatly in colour.
- Texture – different tree species have varied surface and cell textures.
- Workability – some species of tree are much easier to work with than others.
- Structural strength – different species vary from weak to very strong.

Hardwoods and Softwoods

Hardwoods	Description	Uses
Beech	• A straight-grained hardwood with a fine texture • Light in colour • Very hard, but easy to work with • Can be steam bent (i.e. heated in steam and shaped by cramping around a former until cool)	• Furniture • Toys • Tool handles
Oak	• A very strong, light-brown wood • Open grained • Very hard, but quite easy to work with	• High quality furniture • Beams used in buildings • Veneers
Ash	• Open grained wood • Easy to work with • Pale cream colour, often stained black • Can be laminated (i.e. sliced into veneers that are glued together and cramped around a former until dry)	• Tool handles • Sports equipment • Furniture • Ladders • Veneers
Mahogany	• Reddish-brown in colour • Easy to work with	• Indoor furniture • Shop fittings • Bars (I.e. in wine bars / pubs) • Veneers
Teak	• A very durable, oily wood • Golden brown in colour • Highly resistant to moisture	• Outdoor furniture • Boat building • Laboratory furniture and equipment

Softwoods	Description	Uses
Scots pine (Red Deal)	• Straight-grained but knotty • Light in colour (cream / pale brown) • Fairly strong but easy to work with • Inexpensive	• Readily available for DIY work • Mainly used for constructional work and simple joinery
Parana pine	• Hard and straight-grained • Almost knot free • Fairly strong and durable • Expensive • Pale yellow with red / brown streaks	• High quality pine furniture and fittings, e.g. doors and staircases

Manufactured Boards

Manufactured Boards

Name	Description	Uses
Medium density fibreboard (MDF)	• Has a smooth, even surface • Easily machined and painted or stained • Available in water and fire-resistant form • Can be machined • Often veneered or painted to improve its appearance	• Furniture and interior panelling
Hardboard	• A very cheap particle board • Can have a laminated plastic surface	• Furniture backs • Door panels • Covering curved surfaces
Chip board	• Made from chips of wood glued together with urea formaldehyde • Usually veneered with an attractive hardwood or covered in plastic laminate	• Kitchen and bedroom furniture • Shelving and general DIY work
Plywood	• A very strong board, constructed of layers of veneer or plies, which are glued with the grains at 90° to each other • Interior and exterior grades available • A very durable water and boil proof (WBP) plywood that can be used in extreme conditions	• Furniture making • Boat building and exterior work
Blockboard	• Similar to plywood, but has a central layer made from strips of timber • Used where heavier structures are needed	• Shelving and worktops • Furniture backs

Quick Test

1. What kind of fibre is needed to create wood?
2. How is wood pulp created?
3. What is the term used for any paper that is over 200g/m² in weight?
4. Give one use for foil-lined board.
5. Give two characteristics of wood that you should consider when choosing a wood for a particular use.

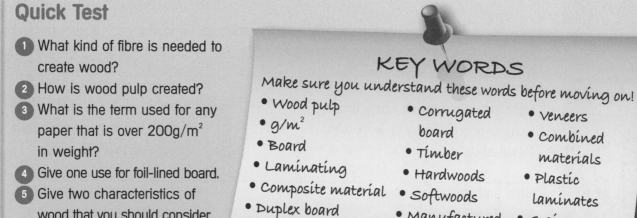

KEY WORDS

Make sure you understand these words before moving on!

- Wood pulp
- g/m²
- Board
- Laminating
- Composite material
- Duplex board
- Foil-lined board
- Corrugated board
- Timber
- Hardwoods
- Softwoods
- Manufactured boards
- Veneers
- Combined materials
- Plastic laminates
- Grain

Metals and their Properties

Metal ore is mined from the ground, and the metal is then extracted from the rocks in a large scale industrial process. There are three main types of metal, but some metals fit into more than one type:

Most **ferrous** metals consist of iron, carbon and other elements. Examples are wrought iron, mild steel, tool steel, stainless steel and cast iron. Most ferrous materials are prone to **rusting** and can be picked up with a **magnet** (the exception is stainless steel, which is designed not to rust and some grades are non-magnetic).

Rusty Iron

Non-ferrous metals don't contain any iron at all, so they aren't attracted to a magnet and don't rust when exposed to moisture (but they do tarnish and oxidise). Examples are copper, aluminium, tin and zinc.

Alloys are examples of **combined materials**. Alloys are metals that contain two or more elements. The elements that make up an alloy may be metal or non-metal. Alloys are chosen for a particular purpose because of their properties, for example their low melting points, corrosion resistance or overall weight. Examples are casting alloy, pewter and brass.

Tarnished Copper

Properties and Size of Metals

Here are some things to consider when choosing a metal for a specific purpose:

- **Elasticity** – the ability to regain its original shape after it has been deformed.
- **Ductility** – the ability to be stretched without breaking.
- **Malleability** – the ability to be easily pressed, spread and hammered into shapes.
- **Hardness** – resistance to scratching, cutting and wear.
- **Work hardness** – a change in the hardness of a metal due to repeated hammering or strain.
- **Brittleness** – breaking easily without bending.
- **Toughness** – resistance to breaking, bending or deforming.
- **Tensile strength** – strength when stretched.
- **Compressive strength** – strength when under compression.

Metals are available in a wide variety of sections, for example…
- round bar
- square bar
- flat bar
- square tube
- round tube.

Many specialist sections, e.g. hexagonal (useful for making bolts), angled and channelled are available in both ferrous and non-ferrous metals.

Sheets are usually sold in **imperial sizes**, but in **metric thicknesses**, e.g. 1mm, 2mm, etc.

Ferrous Metals

Name	Description	Uses
Cast iron	• Re-melted pig iron with some small quantities of other metals • Typically 93% iron with 4% carbon and 3% other elements • Very strong in compression, but brittle	• Metalwork vices • Brake discs and drums • Car cylinder blocks • Manhole and drain covers • Machinery bases
Mild steel	• Iron mixed with 0.15–0.3% carbon • Ductile and malleable • Rusts very quickly if exposed to moisture	• Nuts • Bolts • Car bodies • Furniture frames • Gates • Girders
Tool steel	• Also known as 'medium' or 'high carbon' steel • Up to 1.5% carbon content • Strong and very hard	• Hand tools, e.g. chisels, screwdrivers, hammers, saws • Garden tools • Springs
High speed steel	• Contains a high content of tungsten, chromium and vanadium • Brittle but resistant to wear • Used in machining operations where high speeds and high temperatures are created	• Drill bits • Lathe tools • Milling cutters
Stainless steel	• An alloy of iron with typically 18% chromium and 8% nickel • Very resistant to wear and corrosion • Doesn't rust	• Kitchen sinks and general fittings in commercial kitchens • Cutlery • Dishes • Teapots • Surgical instruments

Non-ferrous Metals and Alloys

Non-ferrous Metals	Description	Uses
Aluminium	• Light grey and light in weight • Can be polished to a mirror-like appearance • Anodised to protect the surface and give it colour	• Cooking foil, saucepans, chocolate wrappers, window frames, toy cars, ladders
Copper	• Reddish-brown, but can turn green after exposure to oxygen • Ductile and malleable • An excellent conductor of heat and electricity	• Plumbing and electrical components • Domed roofs (copper covered)
Tin	• Bright silver, ductile and malleable and resistant to corrosion • Tinplate is steel with a tin coating	• Most commonly used as a coating on food cans and similar packaging
Zinc	• Very weak • Extremely resistant to corrosion from moisture	• Used as a coating on steel buckets, screws and roofing sheets (galvanised steel) • Die casting alloys
Silver	• Precious metal • Very ductile and malleable • Tarnishes	• Jewellery; Plated onto electrical wires to improve contact and reduce resistance

Alloys	Description	Uses
Brass	• Hard, yellow metal • An alloy of about 65% copper and 35% zinc • Often cast and machined, then chromium plated	• Decorative metal work, e.g. door handles, candlesticks and boat fittings • Plumbing accessories
Pewter	• Now a lead-free alloy for safety • Made of 92% tin, 6% antimony and 2% copper • Polishes to a bright, mirror-like finish • Low melting point	• Drinking tankards, jewellery, picture frames, decorative gifts
Casting alloy (LM4)	• Mainly aluminium with 3% copper and 5% silicon • Looks like pure aluminium	• Sand casting • Die casting engine components, especially on motorcycles

Thermosetting Plastics

Polymerisation and Thermosetting Plastics

Plastics are the most widely used materials in commercial production. Different plastics can have very different properties.

Natural plastics include amber (fossilised tree resin) and latex (a form of rubber).

Synthetic plastics (the most common) are chemically manufactured from carbon-based materials, e.g. crude oil, coal and natural gas.

Synthetic plastics are manufactured using a process known as **polymerisation**. Polymerisation occurs when **monomers** join together to form long chains of molecules called **polymers**.

Thermosetting plastics are heated and moulded into shape:

- They can't soften if reheated because the polymer chains are interlinked.
- Individual monomers are joined together to form a massive polymer.
- They are commonly found in resin or powder form (e.g. for compression moulding).

Plastics can be combined with other materials, e.g. card, metals and manufactured timber boards. In resin form they are combined with glass, carbon or Aramid (Kevlar) to produce **composite materials**.

There are biodegradable alternative materials that have similar properties to plastics.

Thermosetting Plastics	Uses
Melamine formaldehyde (Melamine Methanal, MF) • Heat resistant polymer	• Tableware, worktops • Electrical installations • Synthetic resin paints • Decorative laminates
Epoxy resin (Epoxide, ER) • A resin and a hardener mixed to produce a cast	• Castings • Printed circuit boards (PCBs) • Surface coating • Araldite™ glue
Polyester resin (PR) • A resin and hardener mixed together • Polymerises at room temperature • Often reinforced with glass fibre	• Laminated to form glass reinforced plastic (GRP) castings • Encapsulations • Car bodies, boats
Phenol formaldehyde (PF) • Also known as Phenol Methanal or Bakelite • Hard, brittle heat-resistant plastic • Dark colour with glossy finish	• Dark coloured electrical fittings • Parts for domestic appliances • Kettle/iron/saucepan handles
Urea formaldehyde (UF) • A colourless polymer • Coloured with artificial pigments to produce a wide range of different colours	• Door and cupboard handles • Electrical switches • Electrical fittings

Thermoplastics

Thermoplastics soften when they are heated and can be shaped when hot.

- The plastic hardens when it's cooled, but can be reshaped if re-heated.
- Most thermoplastics are available in sheets – 1mm, 1.5mm, 2mm, etc. Some are available as **granules** for injection moulding, **powders** for dip coating, **rods** and blocks.

Polythene (high density) HDPE is a stiff, strong plastic that softens at between 120–130°C. It's used for pipes, bowls, milk crates and buckets.

Expanded polystyrene is soft and spongy and has good insulating properties. It's a low density plastic that is good at absorbing shock. It's used for packaging, sound and heat insulation, and ceiling tiles.

High Impact Polystyrene (HIPS) is a light but strong plastic that is widely available in sheets and softens at about 95°C. It's used for vacuum forming and in school project work, e.g. outer casings on electronic products and packaging.

Rigid PVC (Polyvinyl chloride) is a stiff, hard-wearing plastic. A plasticiser can be added to create a softer, more rubbery material. PVC is used for air and water pipes, chemical tanks, shoe soles, shrink and blister packaging, and floor and wall coverings.

Acrylic (Polymethyl-Methacrylate, otherwise known as Perspex) is a hard-wearing transparent or opaque plastic. It can be coloured with pigments and will shatter if treated roughly. It's used for display signs, baths, roof lights and machine guards.

Acetate is a cellulose-based plastic used for wrapping.

Polyethylene Terephthalate (PET) is a polyester plastic. It's a clear material useful in vacuum forming or blow moulding. It's used for drink bottles and food packaging trays.

Polythene

Acrylic

Quick Test

1. What is the main difference between ferrous and non-ferrous metals?
2. What is the main difference between thermosetting plastics and thermoplastics?
3. Name two common thermosetting plastics.
4. Name two common thermoplastics.

KEY WORDS
Make sure you understand these words before moving on!
- Ferrous
- Non-ferrous
- Alloys
- Polymers
- Thermosetting plastics
- Thermoplastics

Ceramics

Clay

Clay is dug from the ground and used to make products known as **pottery**.

Modern clays are often dried, crushed and then mixed with other minerals and exact quantities of water to get ceramic materials that are consistent in quality and plasticity:

- Clay is normally sold in bags by weight, e.g. 25kg.
- Clay in moist form is called **'body' clay**.
- Liquid clay (often used for decoration) is known as **slip**.
- The ingredients used for colouring and glazing are sold as dry powders.
- Clay generally remains porous unless glazed.

Ceramics

Ceramics are clay products fired at high temperatures, for example earthenware, porcelain, bricks and some tiles, and stoneware.

Ceramics can also include other related materials that share some similar properties, for example, plaster of Paris, cement and glass.

Ceramic materials are...

- non-metallic, inorganic compounds
- often a mixture of several minerals – primarily oxides and also carbides, nitrides, borides and silicides.

Ceramics are often combined with other materials to provide different properties, for example:

- Cement mixed with an aggregate forms concrete, which is a **composite material** with good compressive strength. When reinforced with steel rods, concrete has excellent tensile strength.
- Glass fibre is combined with some plastics (e.g. GRP) or used in enamelling.

Engineering Ceramics

Ceramic products formed from alumina and silicon nitride are strong and can be used for structural applications. Iron oxide particles are the active component in a variety of magnetic recording media, e.g. recording tapes and computer disks.

Ceramics is one of the most advanced groups of materials currently being developed. They're resistant to high temperatures so can be used in a variety of applications, for example...

- spark plugs
- light bulbs
- heat-shield tiles on space shuttles
- nose cones on aircraft and rockets.

Ceramic Materials

Name	Description	Uses
Earthenware clays	• Cheap and available worldwide • Fired at 900–1150°C (depending on clay used) • Porous, but need to be glazed	• Roof and floor tiles • Sewer pipes • Bricks and terracotta flower pots • Tableware and cooking pots
Stoneware clays	• Pale grey in colour turning buff, white, grey or red (depending on clay) • Fired at 1200–1280°C	• General tableware (usually glazed for aesthetic reasons)
Porcelain	• White China clay mix • Fired at 1250–1300°C • Denser and harder than earthenware or stoneware	• Fine crockery 'China' • Decorative vases and ornaments when glazed
Slip	• Diluted clay used in liquid form (chemicals can reduce the amount of water added)	• Slipcasting – a common moulding technique in plaster moulds (small scale and volume production) • Providing decorative details before firing
Plaster of Paris	• White powder mixed with water to form a hard, white stone-like material that is soft enough to carve	• Decorative mouldings • Moulding material for slip casting, dental work and fine metalwork
Cement	• Dry powder mixed with water to create a binding action with other materials • Mixed with sand and water to use as a mortar in bricklaying • Mixed with an aggregate to form concrete	• Building materials
Glass	• Hard, brittle, transparent solid made by melting silica (sand) • Can be made into a fibre	• Bottles and jars • Windows and mirrors • Cathode ray tubes • Light bulbs, spectacles and optical products • Fibres used in GRP and as an insulation material in buildings

Textiles

Fibres

Fibres are the raw materials of textiles. They are fine, hair-like structures available in short lengths or long continuous filaments.

There are three groups of fibres:

- **Natural fibres** come from animals and plants.
- **Regenerated fibres** come from natural, non-fibrous sources treated with chemicals.
- **Synthetic fibres** are made from chemicals, usually oil or coal-based.

Natural Fibre – Cotton

Yarns

Yarn is made by spinning or twisting fibres together. It's supplied by weight and ply, e.g. single, two ply.

To be spun, natural staple fibres (short fibres) must be…

- cleaned to remove dirt and waste
- carded to untangle the fibres to get them parallel and in line with each other
- drawn into a sliver ready for spinning.

The yarn is spun by twisting it anticlockwise (S twist) or clockwise (Z twist). More complex yarns are made by combining S twist and Z twist in equal amounts to prevent distortion.

'S' and 'Z' Twist Yarn

Fabrics

Fabric is usually made from yarn. It can be **knitted** or **woven** into large sheets.

Some fabrics are **non-woven**, e.g. felt. They are made by **bonding** loose fibres together in a process similar to papermaking.

The property of the fabric depends on the fibres used and the method used to construct it.

Fabrics are…

- supplied in standard widths (usually imperial sizes) such as 48", 54", 60"
- sold by the metre length.

Weft Knitting

Warp Knitting

Non-woven Fabric

Plain Weave

Weave
Warp

Twill Weave

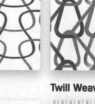

Sateen Weave

Natural and Regenerated Fibres

Name	Description	Uses
Cotton	• A natural vegetable or cellulose fibre • Fibres come from the ripened seed pods of the cotton plant • Strong, absorbent fibre	• Denim, calico, terry towelling, chintz, corduroy, drill, flannelette, poplin, gabardine • Underwear, blouses, t-shirts, suits, trousers, jeans, furnishings
Wool	• A natural animal or protein fibre from a sheep's fleece • A warm, soft, absorbent, crease-resistant fibre	• Felt, flannel, gabardine • Knitted fabrics, sweaters, suits, dresses, carpets
Silk	• A natural animal or protein fibre from a silk moth's cocoon • A smooth, lustrous, strong fibre	• Chiffon, organza, crepe, velvet • Dresses, shirts, ties
Linen	• A natural vegetable or cellulose fibre from the stalks of the flax plant • A very strong fibre	• Batiste • Dresses, suits, trousers • Furnishings
Acetate	• A regenerated fibre made from cellulose (wood pulp) combined with acetic acid • A soft fibre	• Lingerie, underwear • Regenerated fibres are very flexible in their properties and end uses • Can be produced and treated in many ways to create a wide range of properties and fabrics for almost any end use
Viscose	• A regenerated fibre made from wood pulp (eucalyptus/pine/beech) treated with chemicals • Produces an absorbent fibre	

Synthetic Fibres

Name	Description	Uses
Polyamide (Nylon)	• Chemically produced from two different monomers • A strong, durable fibre • Warm and crease resistant • Has good elastic recovery	• Socks, tights and stockings • Upholstery, decorative furnishings, carpets • Lightweight sportswear
Tactel	• Derived from Polyamide • Has the highest strength to weight ratio of any fibre	• Ski wear • Lingerie
Polyester	• Chemically produced from oil • A strong, durable fibre • Elastic and crease resistant • Combines well with other fibres	• Sportswear • Cotton and polyester terry towels (lightweight and quick-drying)
Acrylic	• Chemically produced from oil • Similar to wool • A very soft and warm fibre	• Clothing, fake fur, knitted velvets, single jersey • Furnishings
Elastane (Lycra)	• A polyurethane fibre • Strong and extremely elastic • Can be stretched up to 7 times its length and instantly recovers its initial length • Combines well with other fibres (produces a stretchy fabric that holds its shape)	• Knitted and woven fabric • Underwear • Sports clothing • Fashion garments

Quick Test

1. How is clay turned into a ceramic?
2. Name two common natural fibres.
3. Name two common synthetic fibres.
4. How can glass and plastic be combined to make a composite material?

KEY WORDS

Make sure you understand these words before moving on!

- Clay
- Pottery
- Body clay
- Slip
- Ceramics
- Composite material
- Slipcasting
- Natural fibres
- Regenerated fibres
- Synthetic fibres
- Yarn
- Woven/non woven fabrics

Food Groups

Food materials can be classified into five main groups, and a healthy diet requires a **balance** of these food groups. For example, carbohydrates should make up about 32% of an adult's daily intake of food, whilst fat and sugars should only make up a small proportion.

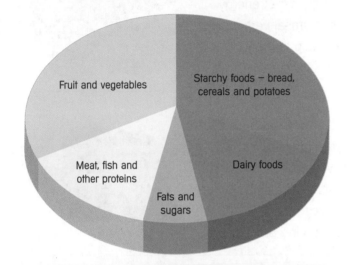

The different food groups contain different things:

- **Proteins** are needed for body growth and repair.
- **Fats** are needed for energy and to keep the body healthy.
- **Carbohydrates** are needed to provide energy and work with proteins to aid growth and repair.
- **Vitamins** are needed to prevent illness and control the release of energy in the body.
- **Minerals** are needed to help in building the body and controlling how it works.

Most food ingredients are supplied in weight or volume, for example...

- grams
- litres.

Healthy Eating

You should think about the **nutritional** value of the food materials used in manufacturing food products. Healthier option food products are now very popular.

The government has produced **guidelines** to help people maintain a **balanced** diet, including...

- eat a variety of different foods
- eat the right amount to be a healthy weight for your height
- eat plenty of foods rich in starch and fibre
- don't eat too many fatty or sugary foods
- store and prepare foods carefully so that their vitamins and minerals aren't lost.

The '**five a day**' campaign is aimed at educating everyone to eat five portions of fruit or vegetables as part of a healthy lifestyle. Fruit and vegetables are...

- packed with vitamins and minerals
- can help you maintain a healthy weight
- an excellent source of fibre and antioxidants.

Food Groups

Food Group	Description and Healthy Eating Tips
Bread, cereals and potatoes • Pasta, rice, noodles, beans, pulses (e.g. lentils), oats, flour, breakfast cereals • Provide starchy carbohydrates and fibre	• Makes up a large proportion of a healthy diet • A good source of energy • Use wholemeal versions as they contain more fibre
Fruit and vegetables • Frozen, fresh, dried and canned fruit and vegetables, fruit juices • Contain lots of vitamins and fibre	• Makes up a large proportion of a healthy diet • Leafy vegetables provide iron • Better to eat fresh fruits and vegetables as some vitamins are lost during processing
Milk and dairy products • Milk, cheese and yoghurt • Contain lots of protein, calcium, vitamins A and D and some fats	• Makes up a moderate proportion of a healthy diet • Eat lower fat versions, e.g. skimmed milk and low-fat cheeses
Meat, fish and other proteins • Red meats, white meats, meat products (e.g. sausages, meat spreads and beef burgers), fish (including canned) and eggs • Nuts, beans and pulses • Contain lots of protein, particularly meat, though they also contain fat	• Makes up a moderate proportion of a healthy diet • Reduce the fat by grilling, not frying, and trimming excess fat from meat • The vegetable-based foods are naturally low in fat
Fatty and sugary foods • Margarine, butter, lard, cooking oils, mayonnaise, crisps, pastry, cakes, biscuits, chocolate, cordials, fizzy drinks, sweets, ice cream, jams • Contain large amounts of fat and / or sugary carbohydrates	• Makes up a small proportion of a healthy diet • Use more polyunsaturated fats, e.g. olive oil • Use low fat or low sugar alternatives

Properties of Food Materials

Food products are often **combined materials**. It's important to understand how ingredients react when they are combined or processed in a variety of ways.

Food can be given a light texture by **aeration**:

- Whipped egg white traps air and can be folded into a mousse to give it a light bubbly texture.
- Beating margarine and sugar together traps air when making a cake.

Food can be **thickened** or set using eggs and starches, e.g. cornflour, arrowroot:

- Egg coagulates (goes solid) when cooked and can be used to set a quiche.
- Starch thickens when heated and can be used to make sauces and custards.
- Modified starches will thicken without heat and are used in packet mousses.

Shortening means making a food 'crumbly' by using fat:

- Rubbing fat into flour when making pastry prevents the flour from forming a protein network when water is added.

Binding happens when dry materials, e.g. flour and sugar, are **bound** (stuck together) using wet materials, e.g. eggs, milk or water. Several food products can be bound:

- Meat products, e.g. burgers.
- Baked products, e.g. pastry and scones.

Colour can improve the appearance of food:

- When sugar is heated it becomes liquid and turns brown (**caramelisation**).
- Beetroot or other strongly-coloured fruit or vegetables can colour food.

The **flavour** and aroma can be improved with herbs, spices, sugar, fruit or vegetables:

- Chillies create a strong, hot flavour.

An **emulsifier** stops fat or oil separating from a mixture. Egg yolk (lecithin) is often used:

- Egg is added to salad dressings such as mayonnaise.
- Emulsifiers are used in cakes, chocolate and margarine.

Quick Test

1. In which food group are carbohydrates mainly found?
2. What does the body need proteins for?
3. Which two food groups should make up the largest proportion of your diet?
4. What does an emulsifier do?

KEY WORDS

Make sure you understand these words before moving on!

- Proteins
- Fats
- Carbohydrates
- Vitamins
- Minerals
- Aeration
- Thickener
- Shortening
- Bound
- Caramelisation
- Flavour
- Emulsifier

Components

Standard Components

Pre-manufactured standard components can be found in many products and industries. These components are mass produced by specialist manufacturers.

Advantages include:
- They are **cheap** to buy and products can be more quickly and easily assembled.
- The **consistency** and **quality** of products can be maintained.

Disadvantages include:
- Producers who buy in components are dependent on their suppliers and need to check the quality of these components.
- There could be a shortage of specialised components, e.g. computer chips.

Textile and Food Industry Components

Textile manufacturers use standard components...
- to securely fasten and unfasten parts of the product
- as a decorative feature.

Fasteners include Velcro, buttons, zips and press studs. Part-made items are also used, e.g. collar stiffeners, embroidered decals, sequins and beads.

The food industry uses many different components, for example...
- ready-made sauces, herbs and spices
- washed and prepared vegetables
- ready-made pastry
- part-made items, e.g. pizza bases, icing decorations.

Vehicle and Furniture Components

Car manufacturing industries use many standard components that can often be used for different makes and models, for example...
- nuts and bolts
- fan belts, batteries and alternators
- seatbelts and tyres.

In the furniture industry it's often the style of components that marks the different designs. Standard components used include...
- screws, hinges and handles
- drawer runners and feet
- knock-down fittings.

Control Components

Electronic and mechanical components are used to control the operation of a product.

For example, in a car there are control components that form separate and interlinked systems.

The electronics, mechanisms and hydraulics work together to power the engine, transmission, ignition, braking, electrics, steering and suspension.

LONSDALE

FREE

ESSENTIALS

GCSE Design & Technology
Product Design
Controlled Assessment Guide

About this Guide

The new GCSE Design & Technology courses are assessed through…
- written exam papers
- controlled assessment.

This guide provides…
- an overview of how your course is assessed
- an explanation of controlled assessment
- advice on how best to demonstrate your knowledge and skills in the controlled assessment.

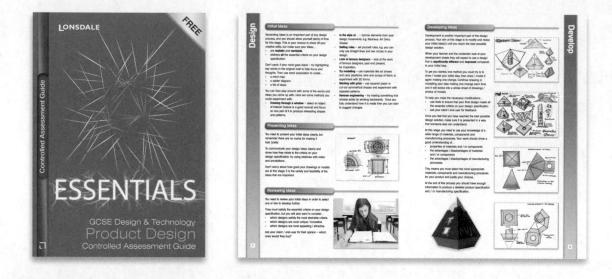

What is Controlled Assessment?

Controlled assessment has replaced coursework. It involves completing a 'design and make' task (two separate tasks for OCR) within a set number of hours.

Your exam board will provide you with a range of tasks to choose from. The purpose of the task(s) is to see how well you can bring all your skills and knowledge together to design and make an original product.

You must produce individual work under controlled conditions, i.e. under the supervision of a teacher.

Your teacher can review your work and give you general feedback. However, all the work must be your own.

How is Controlled Assessment Marked?

Your teacher will mark your work using guidelines from the exam board. A moderator at the exam board will review these marks to ensure that they are fair.

You will not just be marked on the quality of your end product – the other stages of design and development are just as important, if not more so!

At each stage of the task(s) it is essential to clearly communicate…
- what you did
- how you did it
- why you did it.

You will be marked on the quality of your communication too.

Contents

This guide looks at the main stages you will need to go through in your controlled assessment task(s), providing helpful tips and advice along the way.

The Exam Boards and Controlled Assessment

Exam Board	Course	Written Paper	Controlled Assessment
AQA	Full Course	• 2 hours • 120 marks • 40% of total marks Section A (30 marks): A design question based on context, which you will be notified of before the exam. Section B (90 marks): Covers all the content on the specification, i.e. all the material covered in your *Essentials Revision Guide*.	• Approx. 45 hours • 90 marks • 60% of total marks (equivalent to 2 marks per hour)
OCR	Short Course and Full Course (Yr 1)	**Designing and Making Innovative Challenge:** • 6 hours, plus 30 minutes reflection time • 60 marks • 20% of total marks (40% of short course) A 6-hour test in 2 x 3 hour sessions, which tests… • creativity • innovation • practical design • making skills • knowledge.	**Developing and Applying Design Skills:** • Approx. 20 hours • 90 marks • 30% of total marks (60% of short course) (equivalent to 3 marks per hour)
	Full Course (Yr 2)	**Designing Influences:** • 1 hour 30 minutes • 60 marks • 20% of total marks Section A: 3 questions based on designing influences. Section B: 2 questions based on iconic products, trend setters and influential eras and movements.	**Making, Testing and Marketing Products:** • Approx. 20 hours • 90 marks • 30% of total marks (equivalent to 3 marks per hour)

Important Considerations

Unlike your teacher, the moderator will not have the opportunity to see how you progress with the task. They will not be able to talk to you or ask questions – they must make their assessment based only on the evidence you provide. This means that it is essential to communicate your thoughts, ideas and decisions clearly at each stage of the process:

- Organise your folder so the work is in a logical order.
- Ensure that text is legible and that spelling, punctuation and grammar are accurate.
- Use an appropriate form and style of writing.
- Make sure you use technical terms correctly.

Because you only have a limited amount of time, it is essential to plan ahead. The table below gives suggested times for each of the stages.

Remember, these stages are all part of a continuous process, so these times are guidelines only based on the mark allocation and you should produce your own more detailed time plan. You need to divide the total time for each stage between the individual tasks to ensure that you spend the majority of your time working on the areas that are worth the most marks.

That doesn't mean that the other tasks aren't important, but quality, rather than quantity, is key.

You should aim to produce about 20 x A3 sheets, or equivalent, for your folder (10 for a short course or for separate design and make tasks).

AQA award up to 6 marks for clarity of communication throughout your folder. Whilst these marks are important, 84 of the total 90 marks are for the content, so make good use of your time – don't waste time creating elaborate borders and titles!

Stage	Tasks	AQA		OCR	
		Marks	Guideline Time (Hr)	Marks	Guideline Time (Hr)
Investigate	Analysing the brief	8	4	29	6½
	Research				
	Design specification				
Design	Initial ideas	32	16	61	13½
	Reviewing ideas				
Develop	Developing ideas				
Plan	Product specification			55	12
	Production plan				
Make	Making product	32	16		
Test and evaluate	Testing and evaluation	12	6	35	8
Communicate*	Clarity of communication	6	3		
Total		**90**	**45**	**180**	**40**

Analysing the Task

To get the maximum marks, you need to...
- analyse the task / brief in detail
- clearly identify all the design needs.

It is a good idea to start by writing out the task / brief...
- as it is written by the exam board
- in your own words (to make sure you understand what you're being asked to do).

You then need to identify any specific issues that you need to consider before you can start designing the product.

You do not need to write an essay. You could use...
- an attribute analysis table
- a mind map
- a spider diagram
- a list of bullet points.

At this stage it is a good idea to...
- eliminate all the things that you don't need
- make a list of 'Things I need to know'.

Ask yourself the following questions:

- Who will use the end product?
- What will it be used for?
- Where will it be used?
- What sort of shop / retail outlet will it be sold through?
- Are there any cost restrictions that will influence my design?
- How many products would be made if it went into commercial production?

N.B. You need to have clear answers to all of the above before you start designing your product.

Research

Because you don't have very long to conduct your research, you need to make sure it is all relevant.

It should help you to make decisions about all the issues that you identified in your product analysis, so these are the areas to focus on.

Make sure you keep accurate records. You will need to refer back to the information throughout the task.

You should know about the different research methods used in commercial design, but be aware that they may not be appropriate for your design task because of the limited time available to you.

Possibly the most useful type of research that you can carry out in the limited time available to you is to interview the client / end-user to find out what they want from the product.

Questions for client / end-user:

- What product do you want?
- What do you want the product to do?
- How and where will you use it?
- What size do you want?
- What style do you want?
- What do you like and dislike about existing products?

Product Analysis

Product analysis is one of the most useful forms of research. In the limited time available to you for the controlled assessment you are unlikely to be able to carry out detailed analysis and disassembly of existing products.

However, it is a good idea to look at some existing products with your client / end-user to find out…
- what they like about them
- what they don't like about them
- whether or not they are good value for money
- what improvements they would like to see.

You should also consider…
- the life cycle of the product
- whether the product can be recycled

- the effect of the product on our lifestyle
- whether the product is inclusive (or whether some groups of people will not be able to use it).

The purpose of this is to help you produce a product that is better than those already available. It should help you to identify…
- desirable / successful features (features you could incorporate into your design)
- undesirable / unsuccessful features (features to avoid using in your design)
- areas for improvement (areas that you should try to improve upon in your design, e.g. reducing cost, making the product sustainable).

Research Summary

It is essential to summarise your conclusions and clearly explain how the data gathered through your research will assist you. You should record…
- what you did
- why you did it

- what you hoped to find out (i.e. what your expectations were)
- what you actually found out
- how these findings will affect your design ideas.

Client Interview and Questionnaire

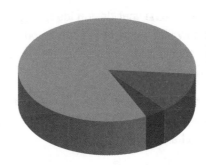
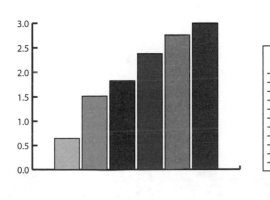
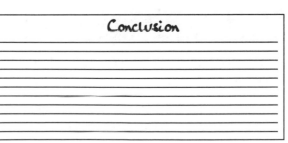

Conclusion

Initial Ideas

Generating ideas is an important part of any design process, and you should allow yourself plenty of time for this stage. This is your chance to show off your creative skills, but make sure your ideas…
- are **realistic** and **workable**
- address **all** the essential criteria on your design specification.

Don't panic if your mind goes blank – try highlighting key words in the original brief to help focus your thoughts. Then use word association to create…
- a mind map
- a spider diagram
- a list of ideas.

You can then play around with some of the words and ideas you came up with. Here are some methods you could experiment with:
- **Drawing through a window** – select an object of interest (nature is a good source) and focus on one part of it to produce interesting shapes and patterns.

- **In the style of**… – borrow elements from past design movements, e.g. Bauhaus, Art Deco, Shaker.
- **Setting rules** – set yourself rules, e.g. you can only use straight lines and two circles in your design.
- **Look at famous designers** – look at the work of famous designers, past and present, for inspiration.
- **Try modelling** – use materials like art straws and card, plasticine, wire and scraps of fabric to experiment with 3D forms.
- **Working with grids** – use squared paper or cut-out symmetrical shapes and experiment with repeated patterns.
- **Reverse engineering** – try making something that already exists by working backwards. Once you fully understand how it is made then you can start to suggest changes.

Presenting Ideas

You need to present your initial ideas clearly, but remember there are no marks for making it look 'pretty'.

To communicate your design ideas clearly and show how they relate to the criteria on your design specification, try using sketches with notes and annotations.

Don't worry about how good your drawings or models are at this stage; it is the variety and feasibility of the ideas that are important.

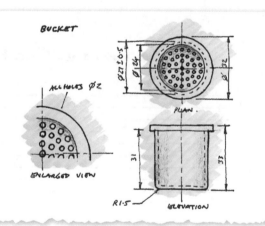

Reviewing Ideas

You need to review your initial ideas in order to select one or two to develop further.

They must satisfy the essential criteria on your design specification, but you will also want to consider…
- which designs satisfy the most desirable criteria
- which designs are most unique / innovative
- which designs are most appealing / attractive.

Ask your client / end-user for their opinion – which ones would they buy?

Developing Ideas

Development is another important part of the design process. Your aim at this stage is to modify and revise your initial idea(s) until you reach the best possible design solution.

When your teacher and the moderator look at your development sheets they will expect to see a design that is **significantly different** and **improved** compared to your initial idea.

To get you started, one method you could try is to draw / model your initial idea, then draw / model it again making one change. Continue drawing or modelling your idea making one change each time and it will evolve into a whole sheet of drawings / photos of models.

To help you make the necessary modifications…
- use tests to ensure that your final design meets all the essential criteria on your design specification
- ask your client / end-user for feedback.

Once you feel that you have reached the best possible design solution, make sure it is presented in a way that someone else can understand.

At this stage, you need to use your knowledge of a wide range of materials, components and manufacturing processes. Your work should show a good understanding of…
- properties of materials and / or components
- the advantages / disadvantages of materials and / or components
- the advantages / disadvantages of manufacturing processes.

This means you must select the most appropriate materials, components and manufacturing processes for your product and justify your choices.

At the end of this process you should have enough information to produce a detailed product specification and / or manufacturing specification.

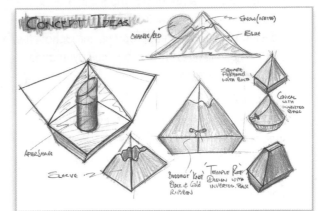

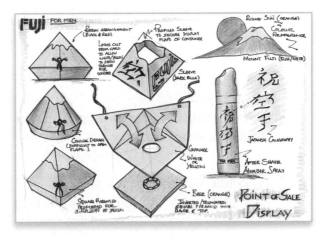

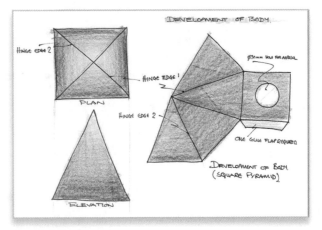

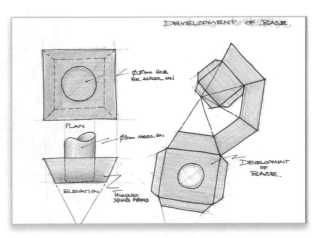

Using ICT

You should use of a **range** of communication techniques and media, including ICT and computer aided design (CAD), where appropriate, throughout the design and make task(s). This is particularly important at the development stage.

This can include…
- standard applications, e.g. Word or Excel
- specialist software, e.g. ProDesktop, ProEngineer, 2D Design and Google SketchUp.
- a digital camera
- a scanner
- a plotter / cutter
- CAD / CAM.

CAD software keeps developing and improving. If it is available to you and it is appropriate, you should try to use some CAD for at least part of your final design.

You might use CAD to…
- make templates
- improve the accuracy and clarity of your drawings
- create numerical data for use on CNC machinery
- make and test scale models / prototypes.

It is vital to include a series of screen grabs in your project folder, so the moderator can see how you used CAD, the changes you made, and how it was used to set up any CAM equipment.

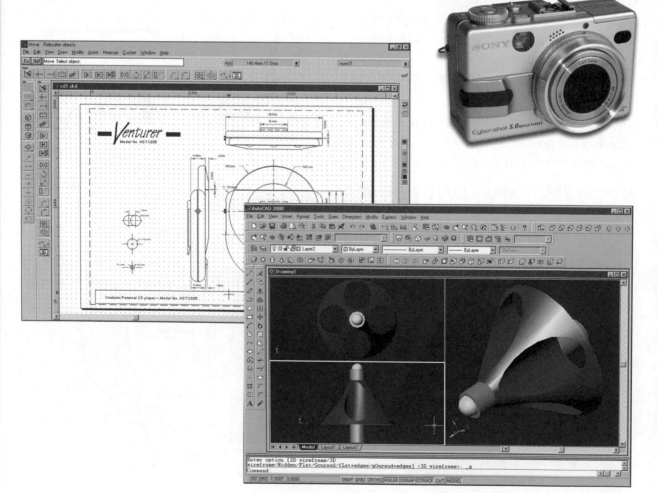

Modelling

Modelling (i.e. making models and / or construction samples) and / or computer simulation is an essential part of the development process. It allows you to…

- check that your overall design works in practice
- trial different types of joints
- experiment with a variety of suitable processes and techniques
- identify and develop support systems to help you successfully manufacture the end product, e.g. jigs and fixtures that can be used to enable accurate repetition of manufacture.

Depending on the size of your product, you may choose to produce full size models or scale models, e.g. 1:1, 1:2, 1:5, 1:10, etc.

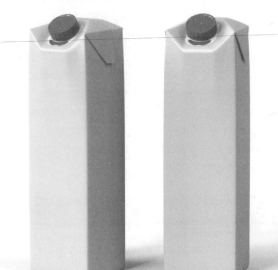

Modelling Materials

Before creating a model, it is important to think about the materials you will use. You must choose materials that are suitable for the purpose of the model and any tests you want to carry out.

Whilst models are extremely useful in helping to develop and finalise your design, you should also be aware of their limitations.

Types of model include…
- card and tape
- foam core
- corrugated card
- styrofoam
- CAD prototypes.

Product / Technical Specification

Your product specification will be more detailed than your design specification. It should include...

- working drawings (drawn, sketched or CAD) – orthographic or isometric drawings, showing dimensions and main construction details
- details of jigs, fixtures and processes to ensure accurate working especially in multiple production, e.g. to ensure that the four corners of a box, chair or unit are all identical

- a cutting list
- a risk assessment.

You should use your product specification to put together a production plan and build and test a prototype of your end product.

Risk Assessment

Look at each process in turn and make a list of possible health and safety risks.

Work back through the list and plan how you will minimise the risks, for example...

- by wearing safety equipment
- by ensuring you know how to use the tools correctly.

Production Plan

Your production plan should show...

- the different stages of manufacture in the correct order
- when and what quality control checks will take place.

A flow chart might be the best way of presenting your production plan, although sometimes a simple chart listing the stages and the equipment that will be used is equally suitable.

If you draw a flow chart, there are different, specific symbols for each stage of the process. The symbols are linked together by arrows to show the correct sequence of events.

You should aim to keep your flow chart as clear and simple as possible.

Flow Chart Symbols

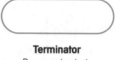

Terminator
Represents start, restart and stop.

Process
Represents a particular instruction or action.

Decision
Represents a choice that can lead to another pathway.

Input / Output
Represents additions to / removals from a particular process.

Flow Chart

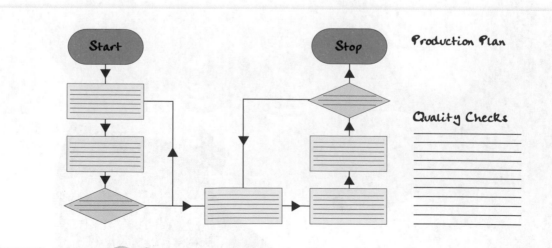

Manufacture

Your revision guide includes information on many of the materials, tools, processes and methods relevant to your particular subject.

In making the prototype of your final product you should demonstrate that, for each specific task, you can correctly select and use all of the following safely:

- Appropriate tools and equipment
- Appropriate processes, methods and techniques (including CAD / CAM where relevant)
- Appropriate materials

You can do this by carrying out the necessary practical processes safely and with **precision** and **accuracy**.

Remember, all the materials, methods and processes that you choose must help to make your product the best possible design solution for the brief. Don't include something just to show off your skills!

Make sure you include photos of your making process.

The finished product should be…
- accurately assembled
- well finished
- fully functional.

Don't worry if it doesn't turn out quite the way you hoped though – you will earn marks for all the skills and processes you demonstrate, so make sure you record them all clearly in your folder.

*For each stage of production, you might want to include…
- a list and / or photograph of materials used
- a list and / or photograph of tools used
- a flow chart / step-by-step description of the process carried out
- an explanation of any safety measures you had to take.

N.B. There are no marks available from AQA for doing this.

Industry

You should have a good understanding of the methods and processes used in the design and manufacturing industries in your subject area.

Although you will probably only produce one final product, it is important to show that you are aware of various possible methods of production and how your product would be manufactured commercially. You should explain this in your project folder.

If your product could potentially be manufactured using several different methods, try to list the pros and cons for each method and then use these lists to make a decision about which method you would recommend.

If you know that a method or process you are using to make your product would be carried out differently in a factory, make a note of this in your project folder – this will show your teacher and moderator how much you know!

Quality Control and Assurance

Your revision guide looks at some of the quality control tests and quality assurance checks used in industry that are relevant to your particular subject (see p.23–24).

Using a jig is one way of introducing quality control in the manufacture of your own product.

Any quality checks you need to make should be included in your flow chart / production plan.

Remember to include…
- photographs of any manufacturing aids used, e.g. jigs
- details of evidence of applying quality assurance, e.g. producing components in quantity.

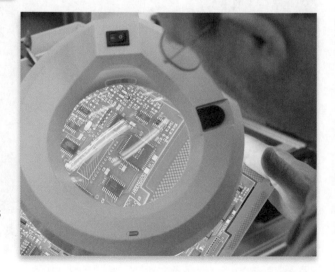

Testing

A **range** of tests should be carried out to check the performance and / or quality of the final product. You need to justify each test you carry out, i.e. explain why it is important.

Tests do not have to be complicated. They just need to be sensible and helpful, e.g. test the usability and functionality of the end product.

When working with food, taste tests are often the best option.

Keeping records is very important. In your project folder you need to…

* explain what tests were carried out
* explain why the tests were carried out
* describe what you found out
* explain what modifications you would make, based on the test results
* include a photo of the prototype in use.

You should not test your prototype to destruction, but it is a good idea to take photos of your product before testing begins just in case anything goes wrong.

Companies undertake numerous tests on prototypes before a product goes into mass production. These can sometimes include testing to destruction. If you think this type of testing is necessary, you should do it at the development stage using models – the moderator will want to assess your prototype so it needs to be intact!

Please place a tick (✓) in the appropriate box for each sample, where:
1 = dislike a lot   2 = dislike   3 = neither like or dislike   4 = like   5 = like a lot

Sample	1	2	3	4	5
Savoury scone					
Tomato soup					
Meatballs					
Cupcakes					

Evaluation

Evaluation is an ongoing process. During the design and development process, every decision you made (providing it is clearly justified) and all the client / end-user feedback will count towards your evaluation.

The final evaluation should summarise all your earlier conclusions and provide an objective evaluation of the final prototype.

When carrying out an evaluation, you should…
- refer back to the brief
- cross-check the end product against the original specification
- obtain client comments and feedback
- take a photograph of the client using the product
- carry out a simple end-user survey.

You need to establish…
- whether the product meets all the criteria on the original brief and specification
- whether the product is easy to use
- whether the product functions the way it was intended to
- what consumers think of the style of the product
- whether consumers like / dislike any features
- whether consumers would purchase the product and what they would be prepared to pay for it
- what consumers think the advantages and disadvantages are compared to similar products
- what impact the making and using of the product has on the environment.

Depending on what you find out, you can include suggestions for further modifications in your evaluation.

Honesty is the best policy when writing evaluations. If something didn't work, say so – but always suggest a way of preventing the same problem from occurring in the future.

Specification Criteria	Test or Question	Results & Explanations
Must hold flat.	How flat did it go?	The height was 77mm which was higher than expected. I forgot to allow for the size of the feet.

Control Components

Systems

A system is made up of three main parts: **Input**, **Process** and **Output**.

Systems often have sub systems, which control the system by using **feedback loops**.

Electronic systems often control mechanical systems, and many electronic systems are controlled by a simple mechanical system, e.g. a switch.

Input e.g. flour	●	Process e.g. mix with fat and water	●	Output e.g. pastry

Feedback loop, e.g. if texture is too dry, add more water

Electronics and Mechanisms

Electronic circuits are usually built from a wide collection of individual components all working together.

Many of the functions of individual components have now been replaced by **Integrated Circuits** (an **IC** or **chip**).

Many integrated circuits can now be programmed to perform certain operations. These are called PIC chips and are widely used in many modern control applications, e.g. mobile phones and washing machines.

Mechanisms are designed to make tasks easier to carry out. They generate a force and movement in a product. They can be used in many products from a simple moving toy to a piece of serious engineering.

When deciding on a particular mechanism to use, you need to look at the…
- input force and movement available
- output force and movement required.

There are four types of movement:
- **Rotating** or rotary (turning in a circle).
- **Linear** (moving in one direction).
- **Reciprocating** (moving backwards and forwards).
- **Oscillating** (swinging in alternate directions).

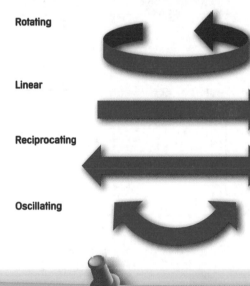

Rotating

Linear

Reciprocating

Oscillating

Quick Test

1. Give one advantage of a pre-manufactured standard component.
2. Give one disadvantage of a pre-manufactured standard component.
3. What are the four parts that make up any system?
4. List the four types of mechanical movement.

KEY WORDS

Make sure you understand these words before moving on!
- Pre-manufactured standard components
- Specialised
- Input
- Process
- Output
- Feedback loop
- Integrated circuit
- Programmable integrated circuit
- Mechanisms
- Rotating
- Linear
- Reciprocating
- Oscillating

Electronic Components

Name and Symbol	Description	Uses
Battery (power cell)	• Measured in volts	• Used to power components and products • Provides the energy to a circuit
Switches	• Used in many circuits to switch parts of the circuit on and off • A large selection available, including push to make, push to break, toggle, slide, latching	• The most common method of activating electrical products
Transistors	• Semi-conductors • Have three connections termed collector, base and emitter	• Electronic switches where a small current is used to switch on a larger current • Sensing circuits (sensitive to small currents)
Capacitors	• Store electrical charge • When 'charged up' there is a voltage across the two leads • Available in different shapes and sizes • Specified in units of farads	• Camera flash • Flashing lights Two types: • Ceramic – no polarity • Electrolytic – must be connected the right way round
Resistors	• Used to control the flow of electric current through a circuit • Resistance is measured in ohms • Can be variable or fixed	• Used with capacitors to control the time it takes to charge the capacitor • Variable resistors can alter the sensitivity of a circuit
Integrated circuits (ICs)	• Complex circuits cut into silicon • Often known as silicon chips or 'chips'	• Created for specific tasks, e.g. timing (the 555 timer is a common IC) • PIC chips can be programmed for many different uses and can replace more complex component-based circuits

Electrical Components

Name	Description	Uses
Filament bulbs (lamps)	• Very simple output devices • Convert electrical energy into light and heat energy	• Torches • Car headlights • Household bulbs
DC motors	• Convert electrical energy into rotational movement • The rotational movement can be reversed by swapping the polarity of the motor connectors	• Driving mechanical devices that provide movement, e.g. fans • Toy cars
Light Emitting Diode (LEDs)	• Available in a range of sizes, shapes and colours • Usually housed in a plastic socket • Must be connected the correct way round	• Indicators to show that circuits are operating • Warning devices (extra bright and flashing LEDs) • High output LEDs can be used for torches (they have low power use)
Buzzers	• Convert electrical energy into a continuous sound • The volume depends on the supply voltage (must be connected the correct way) • No need for an input signal	• Warning devices, e.g. alarm circuits
Loudspeakers / Bells	• Change electrical pulses into sound • The volume and pitch of the output sound depends on the pulses received • Need an input signal	• Devices that transmit musical and voice sounds, e.g. telephones and radios • Doorbells
Solenoids	• Convert electrical energy into small linear movements • Electromagnetic devices	• Electronic locking devices • Part of mechanisms for children's toys

Mechanical Components

Name	Description	Uses
Spur gears	• Wheels with teeth cut into their outer edge • They're specified by the number of teeth • Used in pairs or as groups (termed gear trains) to change the speed or direction of rotation	• Gearboxes
Rack and pinion	• A spur gear (the pinion) usually drives the rack, but it can be driven the other way round • Changes rotary motion into linear or reciprocating motion • An oscillating motion can be produced if the rack is driven by a solenoid	• Drilling machines to move the chuck up and down • Car steering
Worm and worm wheel	• Change motion through 90° • The worm is usually the driver • Has a large reduction in speed and a high torque (twisting force)	• Hand-held food mixers
Bevel gears	• Changes motion through 90° • Gears of different sizes will create a change in speed	• Electric hand drills
Cam and follower	• Wheels with a raised profile • Cams come in different shapes • The follower runs against the surface of the cam and produces a reciprocating motion	• Used in groups (camshafts) to lift valves, e.g. in car engines • Sewing machines (repeated movement)
Cranks	• Shafts that are stepped along their length • By connecting a rod, a rotary motion will produce a reciprocating motion • When driven by a piston the crank will produce a rotary motion	• Car engines • Bicycles
Pulleys	• Can be linked by belts, cable or ropes • Pulleys and belts may have teeth to make sure the belt doesn't slip when in use • Different sized pulleys will give a change in speed • A cross-over belt changes direction	• Drilling machines • Sewing machines

Mechanical Components

Name	Description	Uses
Linkages 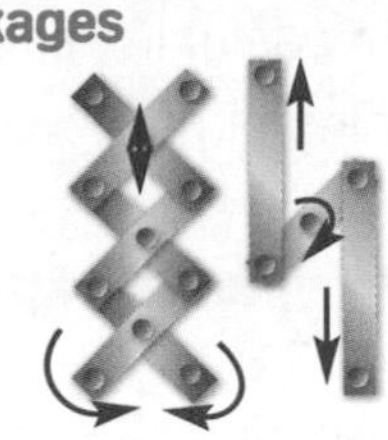	• Transfer motion between mechanisms • Can alter the direction of the motion and / or increase / decrease the motion	• Toys • Tool boxes (used to link trays together)
Levers 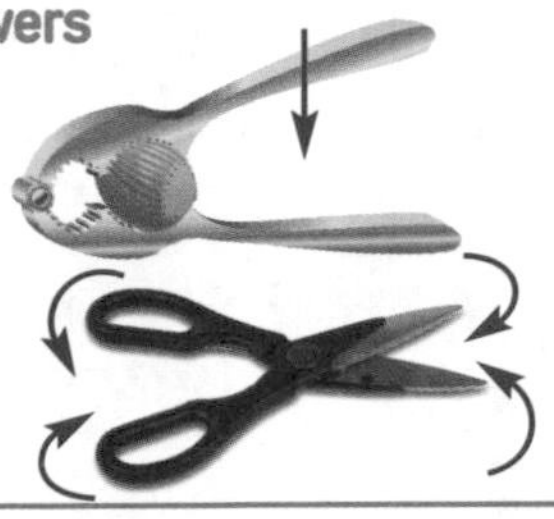	• A simple device consisting of a rigid bar that pivots around a fixed point (**fulcrum** or **pivot point**)	• Used in many hand tools as force multipliers
Chain and sprocket 	• Works in a similar way to a pulley and belt but the chain provides less risk of slippage • Used for reducing / increasing the speed difference between the driver and driven sprocket	• Bicycle chains
Pneumatic cylinders 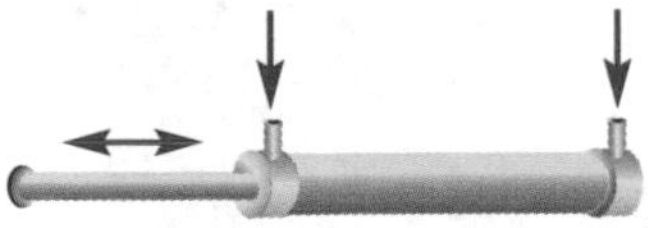	• The most common form of pneumatic component • Provides a reciprocating motion • Controlled by compressed air • Hydraulic cylinders are similar, but are controlled by an incompressible fluid, e.g. oil or water	• Used in a wide range of manufacturing situations including pushing and pulling actions

Quick Test

1. Give one use for a capacitor.
2. What unit is the SI unit of resistance?
3. What is a spur gear specified by?
4. What is a lever?
5. What does a solenoid convert electrical energy into?

KEY WORDS

Make sure you understand these words before moving on!

• Battery
• Gears
• Cranks
• Pulleys
• Linkages
• Levers
• Fulcrum

New Materials

New Materials and Smart Materials

There has been a rapid advance in what are termed **new materials.** These materials have properties that allow them to be used in new and exciting applications.

Smart materials react and change their properties in response to inputs, for example electrical current, heat and light. This makes them useful in safety applications, e.g. to give a warning of heat.

Polymers, Metal Clays and Composites

Starch-based polymers are made from corn (maize) or potato starch. They are biodegradable and don't give off toxic fumes when burned, so are more environmentally friendly than oil-based polymers. They are being used as a safer option in…

*   food packaging
*   disposable products, e.g. cutlery.

The development of **precious metal clay** (PMC) has led to much more creative jewellery:

*   It's made from 99.9% fine particles of metal (usually silver) mixed with a binder and water.
*   It looks and is worked like clay, but when dried and heated to approx. 800°C, the metal particles fuse together and it becomes solid metal.

Quantum tunnelling composites incorporate electronics into textiles. They are metal-filled polymers that can change from an insulator to a conductor when pressed. When squeezed, the metal particles squash together and it becomes easier for the electrons to pass between them.

These composites have been used in…

*   temperature controlled and high visibility clothing
*   space suits that have electronic systems, e.g. iPods built into the suit.

Precious Metal Clay Pendant

Carbon Fibres and Foamed Metals

Carbon fibres can be woven into a fabric sheet and then impregnated with an epoxy or phenolic resin and forced into a mould. The material is then cured (or set) with heated steam to create a very strong lightweight material, used for example in Formula One racing cars, bicycles and sports equipment.

Some metals, e.g. aluminium, can be processed so that it foams. When sandwiched between two solid sheets it produces a material that is lighter, stiffer and more resistant to impact than solid sheet as the foam core absorbs and disperses the energy around the small cells walls. This is particularly useful in vehicle design.

Other new materials that you could work with include flexible plywood, 3D veneers, Polymorph, Necuron foam, Maplex and microfibres.

Smart Textiles and Pigments

Smart textiles are fabrics that react to changes in the environment, for example…

- **thermochromic dyes** allow a fabric to change colour in response to heat
- **photochromic** dyes allow a fabric to change colour in sunlight.

Thermochromic **pigments** change colour with temperature and can be added to polymers. They can be used in kettles and as thermal warning patches in baby feeding products.

Phosphorescent pigments absorb light energy and release it when it's dark. Pigment powder can be…

- mixed with acrylic paints and inks to produce signage that can be seen in the dark, e.g. fire exit signs and clock hands
- added to polymers to create novelty, luminous stars.

Shape Memory Alloys and Nanotechnology

Shape memory alloys can be heat treated so the metal gains a memory. For example, a Nitinol wire (an alloy of nickel and titanium) will shrink by about 5% of its length when an electrical current is passed through it. It can then be stretched back to its original size once the current is turned off.

These **super-elastic** alloys can be…

- placed into collapsed blood vessels or around broken bones (bio-engineering)
- used for spectacle frames, which can be squashed and then return to their original shape at room temperature.

Nanotechnology deals with materials at an atomic or molecular scale and is being used to create very advanced reactive materials and uses:

- Nanomaterials are small enough to enter the bloodstream so they can be used to deliver drugs round the body.
- Food packaging with added anti-microbial agents.
- UV-protective cosmetics.
- Increasing the strength of polymers to replicate properties of metals and making surfaces harder wearing.
- Clothing that repels dirt, stains and body odours and can 'self-clean' with a cup of water.
- Garments that can sense, react and absorb an impact or collision and so protect your body. These can be used in extreme sports or military applications.
- Sports clothing that can measure your fitness levels and create individual training programmes based on your body's feedback.

Quick Test

1. What happens to precious metal clay when it's heated to 800°C?
2. What do thermochromic dyes react to?
3. Give one use for phosphorescent pigments.
4. What will happen to a Nitinol wire when a current is passed through it?

KEY WORDS

Make sure you understand these words before moving on!

- Smart materials
- Starch-based polymers
- Precious metal clay
- Quantum tunnelling composites
- Carbon fibres
- Smart textiles
- Thermochromic dyes / pigments
- Photochromic
- Phosphorescent
- Shape memory alloy
- Nanotechnology

Practice Questions

1 Which of the following plant fibres is usually used for making paper? Tick the correct option.

A Wheat ☐   **B** Flax ☐

C Grass ☐   **D** Sisal ☐

2 What commercial use could be made of a composite material that is solid white board with a laminated aluminium foil side? Tick the correct option.

A General packaging ☐   **B** Fast-food lid containers ☐

C Christmas wrapping paper ☐   **D** Large cartons ☐

3 Give two properties of pine.

a) ....

b) ....

4 Circle the correct options in the following sentences.

A ferrous metal is one that **contains iron / does not contain iron / is made solely of tin**.

An alloy **is attracted to a magnet / rusts / is a mixture of different elements**.

5 A non-flammable plastic is needed for an electric switch. What would be one possible plastic? Tick the correct option.

A High impact polystyrene ☐   **B** Acrylic ☐

C Urea formaldehyde ☐   **D** Epoxy resin ☐

6 Which of the following are ceramic materials. Tick the **two** correct options.

A Plaster of Paris ☐

B Limestone ☐

C Cement ☐

D Stainless steel ☐

7 Ceramics is one of the most advanced groups of materials currently being developed. What are they resistant to? Tick the correct option.

A Very high temperatures ☐

B Breaking when dropped ☐

C Cold air ☐

D Oily liquids ☐

8 Why would a Tactel fabric be a good choice for the manufacture of ski wear? Tick the correct option.

    A It's chemically produced from oil ☐

    B It has the highest strength to weight ratio of any fibre ☐

    C It creases easily ☐

    D It's a heavy fabric that is slow drying ☐

9 Circle the correct options in the following sentences.

Food ingredients are normally supplied in **weight** / **height** and **length** / **volume**. For example, solid foods could be measured in **g/m²** / **grams** and liquids in **litres** / **grams**.

10 Which of the following fasteners would textile manufactures **not** use as standard components? Tick the correct option.

    A Velcro and zips ☐   **B** Press studs ☐

    C Buttons ☐   **D** Hems ☐

11 Why is the style of components important in furniture design?

_____

_____

12 Give one example of oscillating movement.

_____

13 What unit is battery output measured in? _____

14 What unit are capacitors specified in? _____

15 Where would you find a gear train? Tick the **two** correct options.

    A In a household iron ☐

    B In a car gearbox ☐

    C In a car radiator ☐

    D In a hand whisk ☐

16 How are carbon fibres processed to make them tougher?

_____

Manufacturing

Primary Processing

Primary processing turns raw materials into useful standard stock sizes.

For example, durum wheat is turned into pasta:

1. Wheat grains are milled to produce semolina, which is mixed with water to make a dough.
2. Eggs, salt and vegetable oil are added. Spinach or tomato puree could also be added to give flavour and colour.
3. The dough is shaped into the many forms of stock pasta shapes and then dried.

Most manufacturing relies on primary materials before secondary processing.

Secondary Processing

Secondary processing turns standard stock materials into manufactured products or components.

There are six stages and they apply to all materials.

1. **Casting and moulding** is the pouring or forcing of liquid or non-solid material into moulds. Once the material has returned to a solid state it's removed from the mould. The moulds can be either re-used or broken up afterwards.
2. **Forming** changes the form (shape and size) of the material, but it doesn't normally alter the volume. A force is applied to the material, which changes it but doesn't destroy it, for example...
   - air pressure
   - hammering
   - vacuum.
3. **Wastage** (or separation) changes both the size and the shape of the material:
   - **Machining** removes small amounts of the material at a time, e.g. sawing
   - **Shearing** cuts the material to shape using a wide variety of methods, e.g. scissors
4. **Conditioning** changes the internal properties of a material, e.g. making it stronger or more elastic. Conditioning is often done using...
   - heat
   - chemical action
   - mechanical action.
5. **Assembling** (or addition) means joining materials together. This can be done...
   - through bonding, e.g. welding and adhesives
   - using mechanical fastenings, e.g. rivets, screws, nuts and bolts.
6. **Finishing** deals with the surface finish of a material. This can be done by...
   - applying some form of coating, e.g. paint
   - changing the surface through chemical action to make a protective or decorative finish, e.g. anodising aluminium
   - electro-plating using chrome, silver or gold.

Scales of Production

It's important that you are aware of the various possible methods of production and how products can be produced commercially.

In a **'one-off' production** only one product is made at a particular time. These productions usually take a long time and the product is often expensive. Examples: sculptures and wedding dresses.

In **batch production** a series of identical products are made together in either small or large quantities. Once made, another series of products may be produced using the same equipment and workforce. Examples: furniture and bread.

Mass production involves the product going through various stages on a production line where the workers at a particular stage are responsible for a certain part of the product. The product is usually produced in large numbers for days or even weeks and will be relatively cheap, but production could be halted if a problem occurs at any stage of the production line. Examples: cars and electrical goods.

In a **continuous production** the product is continually produced over a period of hours, days or even years ('24/7'). The product will be relatively cheap. Examples: soft drinks and wood screws.

In a **'just-in-time' (JIT) production** the component parts arrive at the factory precisely when they're needed. Expensive warehousing costs are saved as less storage space is needed. But, if the supply of components is stopped, the production line is interrupted, which is very costly. Example: cars.

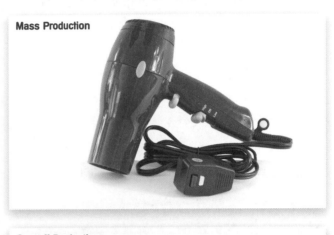

Mass Production

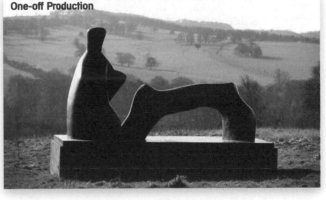

One-off Production

Quick Test

1. What is the purpose of primary processing?
2. Which secondary processing stage deals with changing the properties of a material?
3. Give one example of a product produced by batch production.
4. What type of production would you use to make tins of soup?

KEY WORDS

Make sure you understand these words before moving on!

- Primary processing
- Secondary processing
- Moulding / Casting
- Forming
- Wastage
- Conditioning
- Assembly
- Finishing
- 'One-off' production
- Batch production
- Mass production
- Continuous production
- 'Just in Time'

Computer Technology

ICT and Remote Manufacturing

The improvements and increased use of Information and Communications Technology (ICT) means that most commercial manufacturing is much more sophisticated than any manufacturing you will be able to do in school.

It's now common for all the different manufacturing functions to be combined into a fully automated series of systems.

Manufacturing can be done **remotely**, which means that the designer and manufacturer can be in different locations.

For example, design and manufacturing specifications, complete with digital photos or illustrations, are often sent to printers electronically (via ISDN lines). You could send your designs to city learning centres to have them manufactured.

Email and **video conferencing** makes it easy to monitor production and keep in contact.

CAM, CNC and CAD

Computer aided manufacturing (CAM) uses numerical data called machine code. Machinery used for CAM is often called **computer numerical control (CNC)**. Drawings are created using **computer aided design (CAD)** packages so the term CAD/CAM is often used to describe the process.

The machine code is now created by software rather than being input on a keyboard. This is known as **post processing**.

Computer aided design and manufacture is used in both schools and industry. You need to be able to explain how you could manufacture products in quantity using CAD / CAM systems.

Stereo lithography is used when manufacturing rapid prototypes.

The main benefits of CAD / CAM in commercial manufacturing are...

- accuracy – machines can even check their own accuracy during production
- repeatability with identical components being produced
- easy storage and retrieval of data (a paperless system)
- quick changes / set-ups between different operations
- reduced labour costs
- flexibility – some machines can automatically detect the component and change the machining operation accordingly
- full automation capability with no human intervention necessary.

Electronic Product Definition

Electronic product definition (EPD) allows for all product and processing data to be stored electronically in one large database. All departments working on a project, i.e. accounts, suppliers, analysis, sales, design and production, can then access the information and everyone is kept aware of any changes or amendments.

Manufacturing

Commercial manufacturing consists of a system or group of sub-systems that require the following:

- Special buildings or places of work.
- Information systems to help people communicate reliably.
- The organisation of people, materials, tools and equipment.
- Transportation of materials and finished products.
- The design and production of many products in a systematic way.
- Ways of changing the shape and form of raw materials to increase their usefulness.
- Ways of using tools and equipment to transform the materials into products.
- Quality assurance procedures with quality checks being made.
- Efficient and safe working methods.
- Ways of disposing of waste in an environmentally friendly way.

Health, Safety and Risk Assessment

Health and safety systems protect everyone. In manufacturing industries these systems are continually checked and monitored.

It's very important that you know what health and safety systems are in place in order to protect yourself as well as other people:

- Always clear away your mess (a clean area is a safer one).
- Make sure you know what safety equipment you need to wear.
- Do you know where to put the waste? Disposing of waste carefully can reduce the risk of fire or environmental problems.
- Check out fire procedures, e.g. do you know where the fire exits are or what the different extinguishers are for?

- Don't lift heavy items.
- Do you know what to do if there is an accident, e.g. who would you tell?

Risk assessment looks at the likelihood of problems arising from every activity. When manufacturing a product, you need to do a risk assessment for all stages of design and making.

Quality Assurance Systems

Quality Assurance and Quality Control

Quality assurance (QA)...
- checks the systems that make the products (before, during and after manufacture)
- makes sure that consistency is achieved
- makes sure that a product meets the required standards.

In many quality assurance systems, staff are trained to monitor the equipment, materials and processess they are using in the manufacturing process.

The customer is an important part of any QA system and can be involved in the monitoring at various stages.

You need to be able to recognise symbols and signs relating to quality assurance that are endorsed by recognised authorities.

Quality control (QC) guarantees the accuracy of a product. It is a series of checks carried out on a product as it's made. The checks make sure that each product meets a specific standard and could include...
- dimensional accuracy
- taste
- material quality
- electrical safety / continuity
- flammability tests.

Testing is an important part of the manufacture of a product and can take place at any time during production. For example, an injection-moulded plastic bottle top could be tested after ten, a thousand or a million have been produced. Some of the tests would include checking the bottle top's diameter, thickness and whether it screws onto the container properly.

Tolerances

When products are produced in large quantities, it's very hard to guarantee that each one will meet the specifications accurately. A **tolerance** has to be accepted that specifies the minimum and maximum measurements.

The analysis of tolerance tests can...
- signal the imminent failure of a machine or a tool
- help to achieve the ultimate aim of quality control, which is **zero faults**.

Quick Test

1. What do the letters CAM stand for?
2. What is the benefit of **electronic product definition**?
3. What do the letters QA stand for?
4. Give two properties that QC could check for.

KEY WORDS
Make sure you understand these words before moving on!
- Remote manufacturing
- CAM
- CNC
- CAD
- Electronic product definition
- Risk assessment
- Quality assurance
- Quality control
- Tolerance

Moulding Food

The simplest form of **casting / moulding** is used for food products, e.g. chocolate, sweets and jelly.

- Jelly contains gelatine (a setting agent). The fruit juice and gelatine mixture is heated and poured into an aluminium or plastic mould. Once cool the set jelly can be emptied from the mould.

- Chocolate is slowly heated in a *bain marie* and then placed in a plastic mould.

You can make your own moulds by vacuum forming plastic sheet. Use food-grade polystyrene sheet, but always sterilise before use.

Split Pattern Sand Casting

Sand casting is used to shape metals, e.g. cast iron, aluminium and brass.

The following method, which is common in schools, is almost identical to the industrial process:

1. A pattern is made from a timber, e.g. MDF or Jelutong. The pattern is made in two halves and attached to a board.
2. The pattern is sandwiched between open boxes called a **cope and drag**.
3. A special, oil-bound sand is used to fill each box. One of the boxes also contains two tapered wooden pegs or **sprues**, which form the pouring spout (**runner**) and the **riser** to let the air out.

4. The pattern is removed and the space left is filled with molten metal.

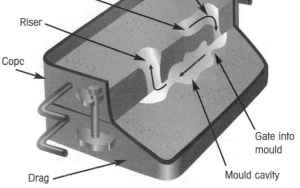

Lost Pattern Casting

Lost pattern casting is used to form metals, e.g. aluminium, into forms that aren't easily achieved using split pattern casting.

The following method is used:

1. A pattern is made from polystyrene foam.
2. The foam is buried in the sand and pouring spouts and risers are added.
3. The molten metal is poured into the mould and instantly burns away the polystyrene foam. The space left is filled with hot metal that's been poured into the cavity.

Toxic fumes are produced using this method and they must be **extracted**.

Lost wax casting is a more sophisticated version of lost pattern casting. It uses wax, which is melted before the silver or gold is cast. It's used by jewellers to produce rings and brooches.

Die Casting and Slip Casting

Industrial Die Casting

Die casting is very similar to injection moulding. It is used to manufacture large quantities of metal products. Alloys with a low melting point, e.g. pewter, aluminium and zinc alloys can be used.

The mould is created by a spark eroding the form required into two blocks of steel. This mould is water-cooled (like a car engine) in order to control the temperature.

The following method is used:
1. The metal is heated in a **crucible** until molten.
2. A hydraulic ram pushes a quantity of the molten metal into the mould.
3. Pressure is maintained until the metal has cooled enough for the mould to be opened.

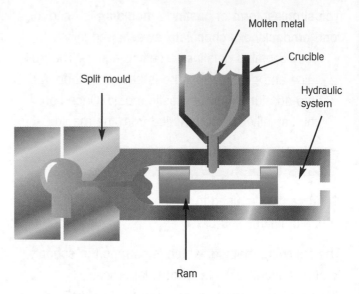

Die Casting in Schools

You can die cast in schools using...
- low melting point pewter melted with an electric paint stripper gun or a blowlamp
- a mould machined out of MDF or blocks of high-density modelling foam (Necuron) cut out either by hand or using a CNC milling machine.

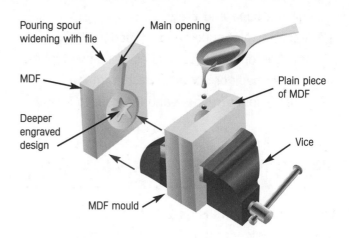

Slip Casting

Slip casting is used to make ceramic products. A plaster of Paris mould is constructed in two or more parts and held together with large rubber bands:
1. The liquid clay (slip) is poured into the mould.
2. The plaster draws the moisture out of the slip and forms the wall of the casting (the thickness depends on how long the slip is left inside).
3. When a sufficient thickness is achieved the slip is poured out and the casting is left to dry and harden.
4. The mould is then opened and the casting is removed.
5. Once dry, the plaster mould can be re-used.

Injection Moulding

Typical materials used in **injection moulding** are polythene, polystyrene, polypropylene and nylon.

You need to know the following steps:

1. Plastic powder or granules are fed from the hopper into a hollow steel barrel.
2. The heaters melt the plastic as the screw moves it along towards the mould.
3. Once enough melted plastic has collected, the hydraulic system forces the plastic into the mould.

4. Pressure is maintained on the mould, until it has cooled enough to be opened.

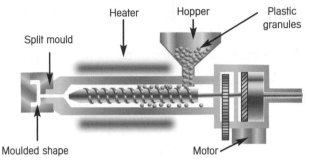

Blow Moulding

In **blow moulding** the plastic is forced into the mould to form a tube, which is expanded onto the side of the closed mould with air pressure.

Another method of blow moulding uses an injection-moulded bottle blank called a **parison**.

This is clamped around the screw thread, heated and blown out to fill the mould. This method is commonly used for drinks bottles because it keeps the bottle neck thicker and stronger.

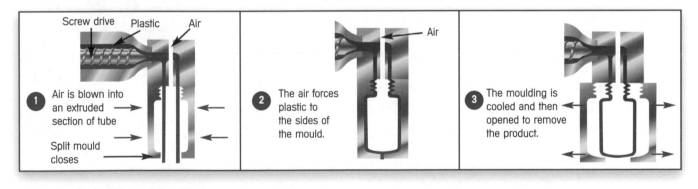

1. Air is blown into an extruded section of tube. Split mould closes
2. The air forces plastic to the sides of the mould.
3. The moulding is cooled and then opened to remove the product.

Rotational Moulding

Rotational moulding can be used as an alternative to injection or blow moulding if making an enclosed object, e.g. a ball or plastic wheel.

A rotational moulding machine has arms fixed at the same point. Moulds are attached to each arm

and rotated continuously with heated thermoplastic powder inside. The mouldings are made from polythene (PE), which can have fire retardant and vandal resistant qualities.

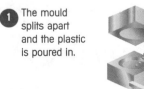
1. The mould splits apart and the plastic is poured in.

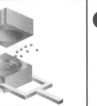
2. Heat is applied while the mould is rotated. The plastic is thrown outwards to the inner surface of the mould.

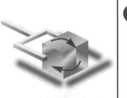
3. On cooling the mould is opened up and the product is ejected.

Forming

Drop Moulding / Drape Forming

Clay is very easy to form in a **drop moulding** process:

1. Sheets of damp clay can be laid across a plaster of Paris mould or former and pressed onto the mould.
2. Any excess material can be trimmed off with a knife or wire.
3. The plaster absorbs some of the moisture and allows the clay to be removed easily.

The same method can be used to form pastry, but a metal, glass or ceramic mould is used that holds the pastry in shape whilst cooking. Acrylic is sometimes **drape formed**. A two-part former could be used.

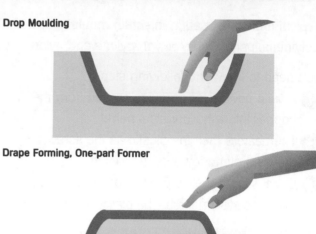

Drop Moulding

Drape Forming, One-part Former

Felt Blocking

Felt **blocking** is a process of forming moist felt (short pieces of animal hair). It is often used to make hats:

1. The damp felt (moistened with water or steam) is pulled over a wooden block.
2. The felt is stretched using hands or simple tools (e.g. rollers) and pinned onto the wooden block until dry.

Hydraulic presses can be used to press the felt over aluminium blocks. This allows large quantities of identical or complex forms to be made in a single process.

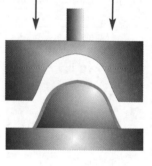

Felt Blocking by Hand   Felt Blocking Using a Press

Vacuum Forming

Vacuum forming uses thermoplastic materials in the form of sheets that can measure up to 1.5m x 1.8m. The most popular material is high-impact polystyrene (HIPS), which is cheap and easy to form.

Heated plastic is 'sucked' onto the shape of **former** required. A former can be a wooden **mould** around which the softened plastic will be held by the vacuum until it has cooled.

1. The plastic is heated and the mould is moved to meet it. Air is 'sucked out' to form a vacuum.

2. The hot plastic is sucked onto the mould. As the temperature of the plastic falls, a rigid impression of the mould is formed.

3. The vacuum pump is turned off, allowing air to enter. The former is lowered, separating it from the final product.

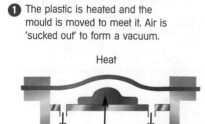

Heat

Air   Mould   Air

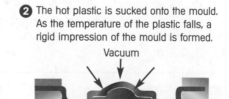

Vacuum

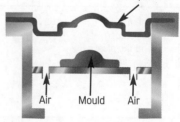

Final product

Air   Mould   Air

Extrusion

Extrusion is a process that produces a material in a continuous section, for example…

- forcing icing sugar through a bag with a shaped nozzle at the end
- producing long 'sausages' of clay using a pugmill fitted with a metal plate that has been drilled with a number of holes
- making plastic drain pipes.

Typical materials used in plastic extrusion are polythene, PVC and nylon.

You need to know the following steps:

1. Plastic granules are fed into the hopper by the rotating screw.
2. The plastic granules are heated as they're fed through.
3. The softened plastic is forced through a die in a continuous stream to create long tube or sectional extrusions (different from injection moulding).
4. The extrusions are then passed through a cooling chamber and cut to the required length.

Aluminium alloys can also be extruded in a similar way to plastics, but the metal is heated separately.

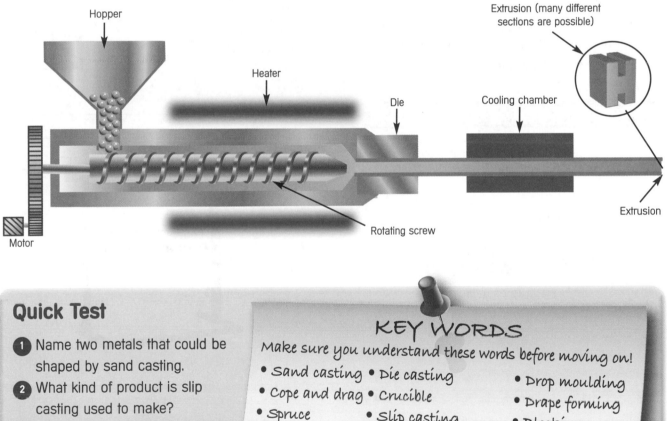

Quick Test

1. Name two metals that could be shaped by sand casting.
2. What kind of product is slip casting used to make?
3. What kind of objects are made by rotational moulding?
4. What product can be made by felt blocking?
5. How does a vacuum former work?

KEY WORDS

Make sure you understand these words before moving on!
- Sand casting
- Cope and drag
- Spruce
- Runner
- Riser
- Lost pattern casting
- Die casting
- Crucible
- Slip casting
- Injection moulding
- Blow moulding
- Parison
- Rotational moulding
- Drop moulding
- Drape forming
- Blocking
- Vacuum forming
- Former
- Mould
- Extrusion

Bending

Bending

Sheet materials can be bent or folded easily. Card is often bent and it can be...
- stretched
- scored
- creased (squashed) before it's folded.

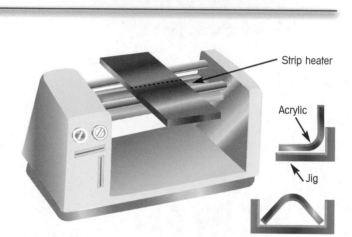

Bending Plastics

Thermoplastic sheets, e.g. acrylic sheets, are often bent using a **line bender** or strip heater:

1. The plastic is heated along the line of the intended fold using a special heating element.
2. The softened area of the plastic is then bent to shape. A jig may be used to produce accurate angles.

Temperature switches, e.g. thermostats, control the amount of heat produced. This allows different thicknesses of plastic to be bent.

Strip heater

Acrylic

Jig

Bending Metals

Sheet metal can be bent in several ways, for example...
- folding bars
- bending machines.

Folding Bars

Sheet Metal Folding Machine

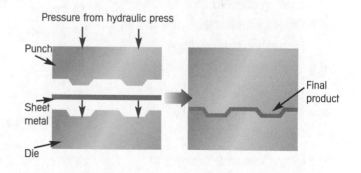

Pressing

In industry, presses are used to bend and form sheet metal (**pressing**), e.g. car body panels and central heating radiators.

Presses are controlled by hydraulic rams, which create massive pressure. Sheet metal is stamped and pressed cold.

Pressure from hydraulic press

Punch

Sheet metal

Die

Final product

Hand Forging

Iron and steel can be heated until they soften. The metal can then be reformed by applying force from a hammer or press. This process is known as **forging**.

Shaping by forging rather than machining ensures that the grain follows the shape of the mould, so forged components are much stronger.

Traditionally, blacksmiths forge metals using...
- a hearth to heat the iron or steel
- an anvil to withstand the hammer blows.

By bending, twisting and hammering, a wide variety of forms can be produced.

Drop Forging

Industrial forging is done by a process called **drop forging** or **die forging**:

1. A piece of white hot metal is placed between two dies.
2. A very large force is applied in a single blow by a mechanical hammer.

1. Heated soft metal — Die — Die
2. Finished component

Compression Moulding

Thermosetting plastics are moulded using **compression moulding**. Once formed, they can't be re-formed. Phenol, urea and melamine formaldehyde are plastics that are moulded in this way.

A large force is used to squash a cube of polymer into a heated mould. The cube of polymer is in the form of a powder, known as a 'slug'.

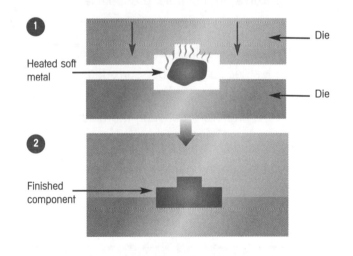

Slug — Hydraulic press — Final product

Mould before being heated — The moulds heat up and are pressed together... — ...to form the final product

Shearing and Die Cutting

Shearing

Shearing is the cutting or slicing action of a knife blade against a shear edge or two blades that cross, e.g. scissors.

Sheet metal is usually cut using a shearing action:
- **Tinsnips** are used to cut small pieces of sheet metal.
- **Compressed air shears** are used in factories.
- **Bench-mounted** shears provide more leverage.

Other materials are cut using a shearing action, for example…
- scissors use the classic shearing action (fabric scissors are often called 'shears')
- food processors provide a **high-speed** shearing action.

Tinsnips

Bench-Mounted Shears

Scissors

Die Cutting

Die cutting works on a simple 'press-knife' principle, e.g. a pastry cutter.

Die cutting is used to cut sheet materials, e.g. card, fabrics and leather. Foam rubber surrounds the blade and is compressed during cutting. It's used to release the material from between the blades.

Die cutting is also known as…
- forme cutting (in the packaging industry)
- press-knife cutting.

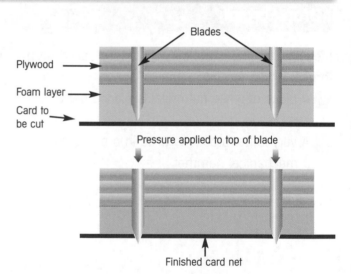

Blades

Plywood

Foam layer

Card to be cut

Pressure applied to top of blade

Finished card net

Die Cutting in School

You can manufacture your own simple die-cutting tools using MDF blocks to hold the blade in place. Making manufacturing aids like these will increase your understanding of manufacturing in quantity, e.g. working to **tolerance**.

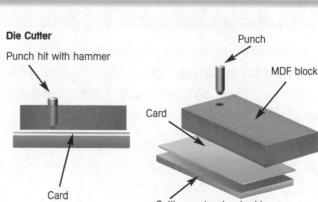

Die Cutter

Punch hit with hammer

Punch

MDF block

Card

Card

Cutting mat or hard rubber

Hand Saws

Most hand-powered **saws** work on forward strokes, but the coping saw cuts on the pull stroke.

Saws have triangular-shaped teeth so they remove a small amount of material on the forward stroke. Ideally, at least three teeth should be on the material at any time.

Different saws are used for different materials and tasks:

- Wood-cutting saws often have the handle fixed directly to the blade.
- Blades are sometimes held in tension within a frame (a coping saw blade can be changed easily when it becomes worn or damaged).

Power Saws

Powered saws use several different movements:

- **Circular saws** rotate and the material is moved across the blade (cuts timber and plastic).
- **Powered hacksaws** use a forwards / backwards motion that is driven by a crank slider mechanism.
- **Bandsaws** rotate a continuous strip of saw blade (cuts timber, plastic and thin sheet metals).
- **Jigsaws** move the blade up and down (reciprocating motion). The work is cramped to a bench and the blade is pushed through the material (cuts sheet timber, plastics and metals).

- **Scroll saws** use a reciprocating motion, but the blade is held in tension and moves up and down through a table that can be angled (cuts sheet timber, plastics and metals).

Scroll Saw   Jigsaw

Quick Test

1. What type of material is bent using a line bender?
2. Give two methods by which sheet metal can be bent.
3. Why are forged components much stronger than machined components?
4. What kind of action is shearing?
5. How many teeth of a saw should be in contact with the material at any time?

KEY WORDS
Make sure you understand these words before moving on!
- Line bending
- Pressing
- Forging
- Drop forging
- Compression moulding
- Shearing
- Die cutting
- Saws

Chiselling and Planing

Chiselling Wood

Chiselling uses a wedge-shaped cutting action. Wood chisels are used on timber.

Chisels need a sharp edge in order to slice across and along the grain. There are four types of wood chisel:

- Firmer chisel
- Bevel-edged chisel
- Mortise chisel
- Gouge

There are three basic chiselling actions:

- Horizontal paring
- Vertical paring
- Chopping

Mortising machines can be used to cut deep recesses for joints.

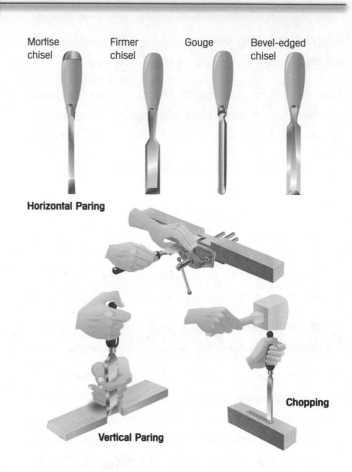

Mortise chisel   Firmer chisel   Gouge   Bevel-edged chisel

Horizontal Paring

Vertical Paring

Chopping

Chiselling Metals

Cold chisels made from tool or high carbon steel are used to chisel metals:

- The cutting edge is hardened and tempered.
- The other end of the chisel is softer to allow it to withstand hammer blows.

Cold Chisel

Planes

Planing is using a wedge-shaped cutting blade to shave off thin layers of wood and some plastics.

Schools may use a **powered** planning machine, which works using a rotary cutter. There are also hand-held versions available.

Smoothing Plane

Drilling

A hole is made by **rotating** a drill or boring bit clockwise as it's pushed into the material. It's important to match the correct drill bit to the material.

- Drill bits (**cutters**) are usually made from carbon steel or high speed steel (HSS).
- Tungsten-tipped **bits** are used for drilling into brick walls, ceramics and glass.

There are many different shaped drill bits that are designed to cut and remove the waste material:

- **Centre bits** and Jennings type auger bits are used with a carpenter's brace.
- **Forstner bits** can be used on timber and some plastics to produce clean, flat-bottomed holes.

- **Twist drills** or jobbers drills are used for drilling smaller diameter holes in timber. They aren't used for larger diameters in wood as they leave a ragged edge to the hole.
- **Countersink bits** are used to allow screw heads to finish flush with the surface of the material.
- **Hole saws** are used for cutting large diameters in thin materials.

Twist Bit   Jennings Bit   Forstner Bit   Centre Bit

Power Drills and Pedestal Drills

Portable **power drills** are available in mains or battery options. They are easy to use, but the material does need to be held firmly in place.

Pedestal drills (also known as pillar drills and drill presses) can be bench or floor mounted. They provide the safest and easiest method of drilling materials.

In industry, several holes can be drilled at once using **multi-headed** drilling machines. Drilling can also take place as part of a computerised machining operation. Thin materials, particularly sheet metal, are punched rather than drilled as it's quicker and neater.

Battery-operated Drills	Mains-operated Drills
Positive Points	**Positive Points**
• No training lead	• Will go on forever
• Can use outside	• More powerful
• Non lethal	
Negative Points	**Negative Points**
• Has to be re-charged	• Limited to supply area
• Has less reserve of power	• Trip hazard
	• Not as safe in damp weather
	• Lethal

Quick Test

1. What kind of chisel is used on metals?
2. Name the four types of wood chisel.
3. List the three basic chiselling actions.
4. What kind of hole does a forstner bit produce?
5. What are hole saws used for?

KEY WORDS
Make sure you understand these words before moving on!
- Chiselling
- Planing
- Centre bits
- Forstner bits
- Twist drills
- Countersink bits
- Hole saws

Milling and Routing

Shaping Materials

Materials can be shaped using a revolving, multi-toothed cutter that moves over the material. This technique is known as…

- **routing** if you're shaping timber
- **milling** if you're shaping metals and plastics.

Routing

Shapes can be cut manually using a powered router. The router can follow a template or be used with a guide to cut slots or to shape the edge of a timber board.

A hand-held router has a guide attached for cutting slots parallel to the edge of a board. This has a variety of cutters that can make different profiles on the material. The cutter revolves into the material.

Hand-held Router

Revolving Cutter

Material

The cutter turns into the material

Milling

A milling machine can move in three ways:
- The **x axis** controls the **sideways** (left to right) movement.
- The **y axis** controls the **front to back** movement.
- The **z axis** controls the **up and down** movement.

The material to be milled is cramped onto the machine bed.

Traditional milling machines can be controlled by moving each axis manually. By moving each axis with a stepper motor very accurate movements can be controlled using **computer numerical control** (CNC). This is one of the most common forms of computer aided manufacture (CAM).

CNC routers are very common in the furniture industry and work on the same principle.

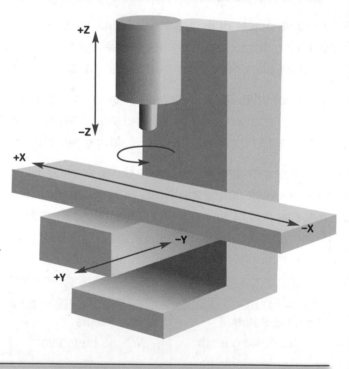

Laser Cutting

Lasers are now commonly used in schools to…
- cut a variety of materials, including fabrics (but not metals)
- engrave materials, e.g. hard plastics and glass.

Laser cutters only remove the smallest amount of material and are very accurate.

Water jet cutting is an alternative to laser cutting and is widely used in commercial production. This form of cutting also only removes a very small amount of material.

Metal-turning Lathe

Turning involves rotating the work against a blade.

Turning metals and plastics on a **centre lathe** involves holding the work (usually in a chuck) and rotating the work towards the cutter. The cutter can be moved left and right (x), forwards and backwards (y).

Five different tools are used – **roughing tool**, **knife tool**, **round nosed tool**, **parting tool** and **boring tool**.

The tailstock can be used to support long pieces of material or be fitted with a drill chuck for drilling holes into the end of the material.

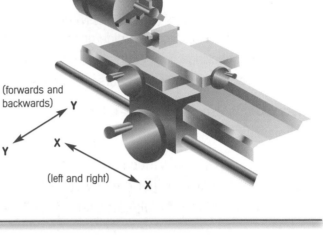

(forwards and backwards) Y

Y

X

(left and right) X

Wood-turning Lathe

On wood-turning lathes, the tool is rested on a support and guided by hand. The work can be held between centres or screwed onto a faceplate.

Four different types of tool are used:

- **Skew chisels**
- **Gouges**
- **Scrapers**
- **Parting tools**

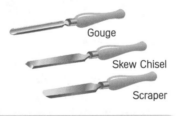

Gouge

Skew Chisel

Scraper

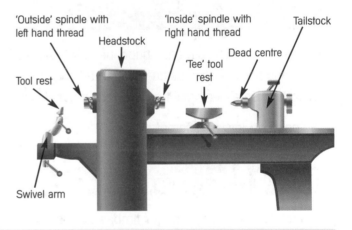

'Outside' spindle with left hand thread

Headstock

'Inside' spindle with right hand thread

Tailstock

Dead centre

'Tee' tool rest

Tool rest

Swivel arm

CNC Turning

The movements of both the work and the cutting tools can be controlled on centre lathes using **stepper motors**. This allows the lathe to be numerically controlled.

CNC lathes are particularly useful for turning quantities of identical pieces.

Quick Test

1. What direction of movement does the z axis control on a milling machine?
2. Give two uses of a laser cutter.
3. Give two uses for a tailstock.
4. Name three metal-turning tools.
5. Name three wood-turning tools.

KEY WORDS

Make sure you understand these words before moving on!

- X axis
- Y axis
- Z axis
- Turning
- Stepper motor

Abrading

Abrasive Papers / Cloth

Abrading works by cutting away very small particles of material.

Abrasive papers are made by gluing small chips of abrasive material, e.g. silicon carbide or emery onto a paper or cloth backing sheet. Each sheet is numbered, and the lower the number the coarser the sheet.

Emery cloth is used on metals and for finishing hard plastics.

Silicon carbide paper is a much finer abrasive paper and can be used either dry or with water (wet and dry). It's used for plastics and cutting back paint surfaces. The water helps to lubricate the cutting action and remove the waste material.

Abrasive paper is usually held around a cork block. Glass and garnet paper are mainly used for timber but they can be used with hard plastics.

Files

Files are used to smooth and shape the surface of metals and hard plastics by pressing and dragging the hundreds of small teeth on the file across the material.

Files come in lots of different shapes.

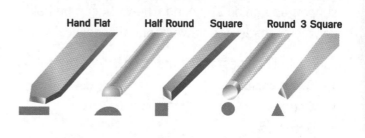

Hand Flat   Half Round   Square   Round 3 Square

Sanding Machines

Sanders are normally used for timber and hard plastics. Sanding machines designed for metals are called linishers.

The abrasive material used on sanding machines is often aluminium oxide glued onto a fabric backing. Fixed sanders work on one of two principles:

1 Rotary or disk sanding:
- An abrasive paper disk is fastened to a faceplate on the end of an electric motor.
- Only the downside of the disk can be used.
- The outer edge spins faster than the middle so material isn't removed evenly.

2 Belt sanders
- Can be mounted horizontally or vertically.
- A revolving belt of abrasive material is powered by an electric motor.
- The belt needs to be supported along its working length by a hard metal surface.
- All parts of the belt move at the same speed so material is removed evenly.

Powered sanding machines create large amounts of dust, which must be safely extracted.

A wide variety of **hand-held**, powered sanders are now available that are both powerful and portable. You should always make sure that...
- the material being sanded is firmly held in place
- any dust created is not hazardous to you or anyone else.

Belt Sander

Cooking Methods

Cooking is the most common conditioning process. It's used to…

- tenderise, preserve or thicken ingredients
- change the taste of foods
- bond ingredients together and change their structure.

Cooking involves transferring heat into the food over a period of time. There are various different methods:

- Ovens use **convection** currents where the molecules in a liquid or gas expand and rise.
- Cooker tops **conduct** heat through the pan's base, which is then transferred to the pan's contents.
- A domestic pressure cooker increases the **atmospheric pressure** (raising the boiling point), which speeds up cooking and reduces energy use.
- Grills use **radiation** where heat energy passes from the grill to the food.
- Conveyor (or tunnel) ovens use **radiation** both from above and below.
- Microwaves use **electromagnetic waves** that vibrate and heat water molecules, causing frictional heat.

Changes During Cooking

Food often changes its structure when it's cooked.

For example, when baking with yeast the following structural change happens:

1. The yeast creates lots of carbon dioxide bubbles and the strands of gluten are tangled together.
2. The carbon dioxide bubbles expand, so the strands of gluten stretch.
3. The gluten sets, which forms the bread structure, and a hard crust forms on the top. Holes formed by carbon dioxide are left in the bread.

Quick Test

1. Why are pieces of sanding paper graded?
2. What would you use a sander for?
3. What kind of heat energy do cooker tops use?
4. What kind of heat energy do grills use?

KEY WORDS

Make sure you understand these words before moving on!

- Abrading
- Emery cloth
- Files
- Sanders
- Convection
- Conduction
- Atmospheric pressure
- Radiation
- Electromagnetic waves

Temperature Changes in Food

Storing and Keeping Food

If food isn't kept in the correct conditions, **bacteria** that cause food poisoning (**pathogenic bacteria**) can rapidly multiply. Bacteria thrive in warm, moist, non-acidic conditions containing plenty of oxygen.

- Temperatures above 121°C destroy all bacteria and spores.
- Low temperatures slow down bacteria or make them dormant, but they don't kill them.

Chilling / Freezing Food

Food can be **chilled** (between 1°C and 8°C) for short-term storage.

Prepared food dishes are cooked and then **cook-chilled** (rapidly cooled to between 0°C and 3°C in 90 minutes or less). They can be stored between these temperatures for 5 days, but must then be re-heated to at least 72°C and eaten within two hours.

Quick **freezing** reduces cell damage in food. Food is reduced from between 0°C and −18°C in 12 minutes and then stored between −18°C and −29°C.

An **accelerated freeze dried** (AFD) food has been quick frozen then placed in a vacuum under reduced pressure. When heated, the ice changes to vapour leaving the food dry. Little heat is used so the flavour, colour and nutritional value of the food remain largely unchanged. These products can be stored at room temperature.

Heating Food

Pasteurisation destroys some pathogenic bacteria. A liquid is pasteurised by heating and holding it at a high temperature for a short time then rapidly cooling it. For example, milk is heated to 71°C for 15 seconds then cooled to below 10°C.

Sterilisation destroys most bacteria. A food is **sterilised** by heating it to a higher temperature and for a longer period than in pasteurisation. For example, milk is heated to 110°C for 30 minutes. This high temperature causes **caramelisation**, which affects the flavour of some foods.

Canning is a form of sterilisation. Food can be...
- packed in cans or bottles and then sterilised
- sterilised and then packed into aseptic (sterile), sealed containers.

For example, baked beans are heated to 120°C for 33 minutes before being cooled quickly.

Ultra Heat-treatment (UHT) is when a liquid is heated to a very high temperature for a short period. For example, milk is heated to 133°C for 1 second. This kills all the bacteria but doesn't affect the flavour.

Annealing and Tempering

Heat treatment is the process of heating and cooling metals to obtain different characteristics. The grains of a metal affect how it reacts to working and cutting. The grain size can be changed with heat.

Annealing is a process of softening a metal so it can be bent or hammered. Different metals are annealed slightly differently:

- Ferrous metals are heated to a cherry red (725°C) for a few minutes and then allowed to cool very slowly.
- Aluminium is rubbed with soap (as an indicator), heated until the soap turns black (350°C–400°C) and then left to cool.
- Copper is heated to a dull red (500°C) and then allowed to cool naturally or placed in water.

Steel can be **hardened** by heating it to above 720°C and then cooling it rapidly in water. This makes the steel very hard (useful in making tools), but it also makes it very brittle.

Tempering reduces the hardness a little but it makes the metal tougher. High carbon or tool steel is tempered by re-heating it to 230°C–300°C and then quenching it with water.

Kiln Firing

Dried clay absorbs moisture and so remains crumbly. By heating (**firing**) the clay in a kiln to 1000°C the particles making up the clay fuse together permanently.

There are two types of firing:
- **Biscuit firing** (950°C–1000°C) fuses the clay.
- **Glaze firing** (up to 1300°C) vitrifies the clay.

Some metal powders are fused together in a similar way. This process is known as **sintering**.

Quick Test

1. Between what temperatures is food chilled?
2. What is the benefit of UHT milk?
3. Why would you need to temper a piece of steel?
4. What happens to clay particles during firing?
5. What is sintering?

KEY WORDS
Make sure you understand these words before moving on!
- Freezing
- Pasteurisation
- Sterilisation
- Canning
- Heat treatment
- Annealing
- Hardening
- Tempering
- Firing

Joining Timber

Many traditional joints are used to build structural strength into products.

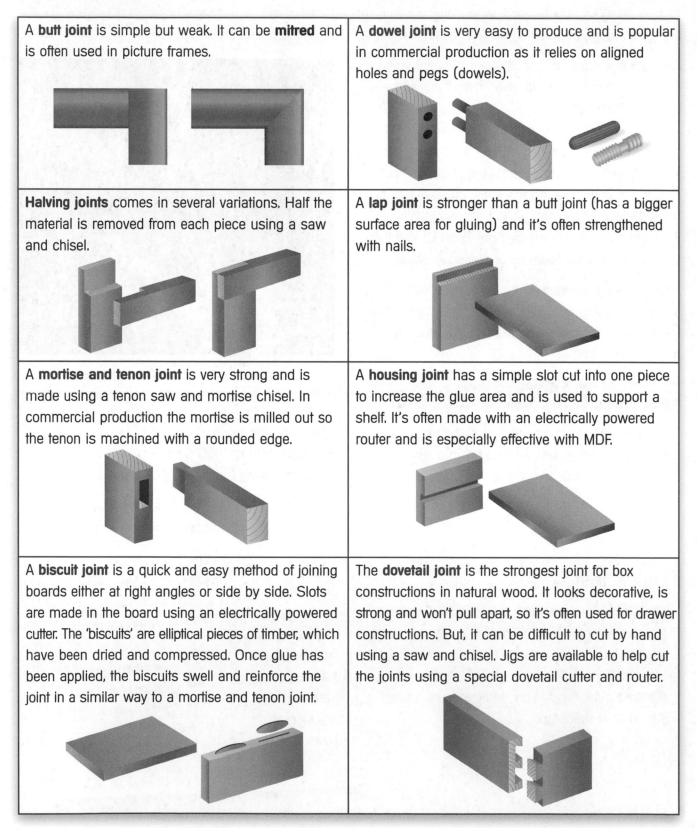

A **butt joint** is simple but weak. It can be **mitred** and is often used in picture frames.

A **dowel joint** is very easy to produce and is popular in commercial production as it relies on aligned holes and pegs (dowels).

Halving joints comes in several variations. Half the material is removed from each piece using a saw and chisel.

A **lap joint** is stronger than a butt joint (has a bigger surface area for gluing) and it's often strengthened with nails.

A **mortise and tenon joint** is very strong and is made using a tenon saw and mortise chisel. In commercial production the mortise is milled out so the tenon is machined with a rounded edge.

A **housing joint** has a simple slot cut into one piece to increase the glue area and is used to support a shelf. It's often made with an electrically powered router and is especially effective with MDF.

A **biscuit joint** is a quick and easy method of joining boards either at right angles or side by side. Slots are made in the board using an electrically powered cutter. The 'biscuits' are elliptical pieces of timber, which have been dried and compressed. Once glue has been applied, the biscuits swell and reinforce the joint in a similar way to a mortise and tenon joint.

The **dovetail joint** is the strongest joint for box constructions in natural wood. It looks decorative, is strong and won't pull apart, so it's often used for drawer constructions. But, it can be difficult to cut by hand using a saw and chisel. Jigs are available to help cut the joints using a special dovetail cutter and router.

Screws and Nails

There are many different types of **nail**, but they make weak joints if used on their own.

Nails or nailed joints are used for...
- holding wood together while glue dries
- fixing the backs of cupboards
- decorative mouldings
- general building and DIY work.

Putting nails at an angle (dovetailing) makes a stronger joint.

Screws are useful for fixing other materials, e.g. metals or plastics, to timber. They can be very strong when used across the grain. There are many different types, but cross-head screws are increasingly used as they're easy to drive in by hand or with an electrically powered driver.

Nailing a Joint   Screwing a Joint

Knock-down Fittings

There is a large range of knock-down fittings for both the DIY and commercial production markets:

- **Cabinet screws** are used to join kitchen units together.
- A **pronged nut** taps into a hole to provide a threaded insert that will take a machine screw.
- A very strong metal-screwed insert called a **cross dowel** sits in a hole and takes a machine screw.
- **Modesty blocks** are available in a range of colours. These plastic blocks are used to take screws in each direction. They are suitable for simple box joints.

Cabinet screw   Pronged nut

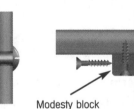

Cross dowel   Modesty block

Quick Test

1. Which is the strongest joint for box constructions in natural wood?
2. Why is a lap joint stronger than a butt joint?
3. Name the wooden pegs used in some joints.
4. What are nails used for?
5. Name one type of knock-down fitting.

KEY WORDS

Make sure you understand these words before moving on!
- Butt joint
- Halving joint
- Mortise and tenon joint
- Biscuit joint
- Dowel joint
- Lap joint
- Housing joint
- Dovetail joint
- Nails
- Screws
- Cabinet screws
- Pronged nut
- Cross dowel
- Modesty blocks

Soldering and Welding

Joining Metals

Metals can be joined permanently by...

- **welding** – using heat to melt a pool of the metals being joined together (like casting)
- **soldering** – using a bonding alloy to form a joint (like gluing).

Soldering Gun

Welding

In **gas welding**, an acetylene torch is used to heat up the joint. A mixture of acetylene gas and oxygen produces a very small, hot flame that melts both the filler rod and the surrounding metal. Gas welding equipment is very dangerous and should only be used in school by trained staff.

Metal inert gas welding (**MIG**) is a form of electric arc welding and is used in...

- schools to weld steels
- production welding using robots.

An electrical spark (which produces a very bright light) creates the heat by arcing between the electrode and the work-piece. The area is cooled and oxygen is excluded with a gas mixture of argon and carbon dioxide.

Spot welding is a form of resistance welding and is used for melting thin sheet steel together, e.g. car bodies. Electrodes (normally copper) sandwich the metal together and a current is passed between them. The resistance creates the heat to bond the two metals in a tiny spot.

Wheels can be used to do a similar process called seam welding. Spot welding is especially suitable for use with robot arms as the process is so easy to control.

Health and safety: You must always wear a visor or protective facemask when welding to protect your eyes from the intense light.

Soldering

Soft soldering joins metal parts together using a lead-based alloy. It's used for light applications. e.g. electrical connections and plumbing joints (a lead-free alloy is used for drinking water joints):

1. Flux is applied to the join to clean it.
2. The metal is heated using a gas torch or metal soldering bit until the solder 'runs'.

Hard soldering or **brazing** is used for heavier applications as the joint is much stronger. The brass bonding alloy (or **spelter**) melts at a much higher temperature than soft soldering. It's used for joining mild steel, but copper can also be brazed.

1. A **borax flux** is mixed to a paste with water and applied to the join to clean it.
2. It's heated to an orange colour with a gas torch and the spelter melts around the join.

Silver soldering is like brazing, but it uses a silver-based alloy. It's used on brass, copper and guilding metal as the bonding alloy melts at a lower temperature than brazing spelter.

Joining Metals and Plastics

Nuts and Bolts

Mechanical joints…
- allow different materials to be joined to metals
- can be dismantled for repair or maintenance.

There are many different varieties of **nuts**, **bolts** and **washers**. Threads are sometimes cut into one of the metal pieces instead of using a nut.

Bolts are made with many different heads including…
- **countersunk head** – tightened with a screwdriver
- **cheese head** – tightened with a screwdriver
- **hexagonal head** – tightened with a spanner.
- **socket head** – tightened with an allen key.

Threads also vary in size, but metric threads are now almost standard in schools (M3 to M12 are the most popular). They are available in many lengths, typically 20–100mm. Smaller bolts are called machine screws and have the thread over the entire length.

Nuts need to match the same thread as the bolt. **Wing nuts** are tightened by hand and are useful for temporary joints. Hexagonal heads are tightened with a spanner.

A washer is usually used under the nut to spread the pressure and protect the surface of the material being joined together. This might be a plain ring washer. A spring washer is often used to stop the nut vibrating loose.

Hexagonal Headed Bolt

Washer

Nut

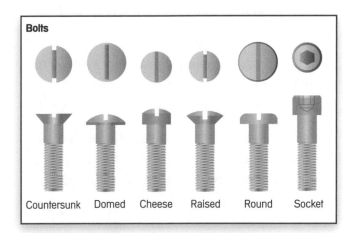

Bolts

Countersunk Domed Cheese Raised Round Socket

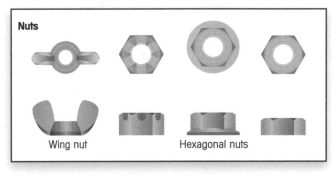

Nuts

Wing nut   Hexagonal nuts

Rivets

Rivets are used to make a more permanent joint than nuts and bolts. They hold the material together by forming a head on both sides of the material. Traditionally, the blank end of the rivet is hammered to form a second head, but **pop rivets** are now more common. They are fitted using a rivet gun from one side of the material.

Rivets come with a variety of heads. They are normally made from soft mild steel, copper or aluminium.

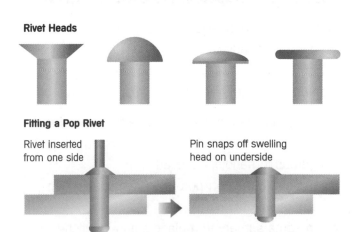

Rivet Heads

Fitting a Pop Rivet

Rivet inserted from one side

Pin snaps off swelling head on underside

Adhesives

Common School Adhesives

An **adhesive** is a compound that bonds two items together. Adhesives can be made from natural or synthetic sources. Adhesives work on several different principles.

Polyvinyl Acetate (PVA) is a white, water-based adhesive. The PVA soaks into the surface of the wood and sets once all the water is absorbed. It's often regarded as being stronger than the wood fibres themselves and so makes a very strong bond.

Synthetic resin is a waterproof adhesive that needs to be mixed into a creamy consistency with water. Chemical hardening then takes place and it becomes very hard and brittle.

There are several types of **solvent cement** available. The most common is Dichloromethane, which dissolves the surface of hard plastics, e.g. acrylic

and HIPS. Very dangerous fumes are given off so ventilation is essential.

Epoxy resin is a very versatile but expensive adhesive that sticks most clean, dry materials together. Equal amounts of resin and hardener are mixed together and it sets chemically to be very hard.

When using **contact adhesive**, both surfaces are coated and allowed to become touch-dry. Adhesion takes place as soon as the two surfaces meet. The solvent fumes are very dangerous and good ventilation is essential.

Latex adhesive is a cheap and safe rubber solution. It does give off a fishy smell, but the fumes aren't dangerous.

Hot melt glue is used for quick modelling, but it's difficult to control so isn't used for final products.

PVA

Hot Glue Gun

Industrial Adhesives

Some modern adhesives are very strong and are used in the manufacturing and construction industries. Many specialist adhesives are manufactured for specific purposes.

Cyanoacrylate is the generic name for **superglue**. It isn't normally used in school as it's expensive and dangerous to handle. It's used …

- to bond hard, non-porous materials together, e.g. metals
- in some surgery to replace sutures (stitches).

Polyurethane (PU) sticks to a wide range of materials. It can expand and take up space between poorly fitting parts, so is very useful in school when prototyping.

Ultrasonic welding is often used in industry as an alternative to adhesives. The molecules in the material are vibrated under pressure and the heat generated creates an adhesive-free bond. It can be used…

- for joining injection-moulded parts together
- as an alternative to sewing with some synthetic fabrics.

Surface Finishes

Finishes

Many materials need some form of surface finish to…
- make them look more attractive
- protect them from deterioration.

Surface finishes can be applied by a variety of methods including brushing, spraying and using a cloth.

Some products are **self-finished**, e.g. injection-moulded products. The mould is highly polished and this means that the same surface is transferred onto each product.

Paints

Paints can be used on metals or timber. They aren't normally suitable to use on plastics, although there are some specialist paints available for plastics.

Paints can be grouped into three main categories.

Oil-based paints usually produce gloss finishes:
- Durable and suitable for both metals and timber.
- The material to be painted must be primed before the paint is applied.
- Applied with a brush or roller.
- Cleaned with white spirit or a turpentine-substitute.
- Normally suitable for use on children's toys.
- Can be used internally or externally.

Water-based paints produce a range of finishes from matt to high gloss:
- Much more available than they used to be.
- Some are only suitable for light use, e.g. matt vinyl emulsion on walls.

- Generally used for painting timber, but some are suitable for metal.
- Less durable than oil-based paints.
- Cleaned with warm water and detergent.

Solvent-based paints produce a range of interesting finishes, e.g. hammered and crackle.
- They dry more quickly than the other paint types.
- Usually available in spray cans (brush on varieties are available, but are difficult to apply).
- Often the most expensive paint type, but can give better results on small products.
- Must be cleaned with the correct solvent (often cellulose based).
- Good ventilation is essential as the vapours produced are toxic and flammable.

Quick Test

1. What is the difference between soldering and welding?
2. What does MIG stand for?
3. What kind of adhesive is latex adhesive?
4. What kind of paint would you use to produce a crackle finish?
5. What kind of paint is the more durable – oil-based or water-based?

KEY WORDS
Make sure you understand these words before moving on!
- Welding
- Soldering
- Gas welding
- MIG
- Spot welding
- Soft soldering
- Brazing
- Spelter
- Borax flux
- Silver soldering
- Nuts
- Bolts
- Washers
- Wing nuts
- Rivets
- Adhesive
- Self finishing
- Paint

Surface Finishes

Varnishes and Lacquers

Varnishes and lacquers are available in oil-based, water-based and solvent-based forms.

Varnishes are…
- clear / translucent or coloured
- available in matt, satin or gloss finishes
- available in spray cans (very suitable for varnishing small products).

Some varnishes have been developed especially for coating metals.

Blue Varnish

Lacquered Rings

Oils and Polishes

Some woods are naturally oily, e.g. teak. Applying teak **oil** or linseed oil to timber…
- improves the appearance of the grain of the wood
- protects the wood for outdoor use.

Vegetable oil can be applied to timber products that are used for food, e.g. serving bowls and salad servers.

French polish is a traditional finish applied with a brush and cloth. Shellac is dissolved in methylated spirits and the finish is built up in layers to achieve a very deep finish. Wax is usually applied on top of the french polish to enhance the shine.

Wood Stains

Wood stains can enhance the colour of a timber and show up the grain patterns. They aren't a surface finish on their own as they need an additional coating of wax or varnish to protect the timber from moisture penetration.

Stains are…
- available in almost every colour, but a colour that is darker than the natural timber should be used
- available in water or solvent-based forms and can also be supplied as stained varnishes
- usually applied with a cloth.

Sanding Sealer

Sanding **sealer** is a solvent-based product, similar to varnish, that is used to seal timber. The quick-drying liquid seals the surface and raises the fibres of the timber so they have to be cut back with fine abrasive paper.

Sealer is suitable as a first coat before applying varnish or wax polish and it works well on top of wood stains.

Plastic Dip-coating and Powder Coating

Polythene is the most common thermoplastic powder used for **plastic dip-coating**:

1. Air is blown through the powder to make it behave like a liquid.
2. Metal is cleaned.
3. Metal, pre-heated to 180°C, is dipped in the fluidised powder.
4. The metal is then returned to the oven where it melts to form a smooth finish.

This process is used for…
- commercial products, e.g. dishwasher racks
- school projects, e.g. coat hooks and tool handles.

Powder coating is a more sophisticated version of dip-coating and provides an industrial finish. The powder is sprayed onto the products, which flow through an oven. Powder coating…
- provides a paint-like finish
- is available in all colours, including translucent
- is very durable.

Anodising, Plating and Galvanising

Anodising is the most common finishing process used on aluminium to provide a durable, corrosion-resistant finish. It involves electrolysis and uses acids and electric currents that are hazardous in school workshops. Colour can be added to dye the aluminium.

Plating also uses electrolysis. There are many forms but chromium plating is the most widely recognised. The thin layer of metal on the surface provides a durable finish that is resistant to corrosion.

Galvanising involves dipping metal (usually mild steel) into a bath of molten zinc. The zinc doesn't provide a very attractive finish, but it's very resistant to corrosion.

Galvanised Watering Can

Plated Cutlery

Quick Test

1. Why would you apply teak oil to a piece of garden furniture?
2. Why is wood stain not a complete finish?
3. What kind of powder is used in the dip-coating process?
4. How would you galvanise a piece of mild steel?

KEY WORDS

Make sure you understand these words before moving on!
- Varnish
- Oil
- Wood stains
- Sealer
- Plastic dip-coating
- Powder coating
- Anodising
- Plating
- Galvanising

Polishing Materials

Polishing

Polishing is a very common finishing method used on...

- timbers
- metals
- hard plastics, e.g. acrylic.

Polishing Timber

A wax polish is normally used on timber, e.g. beeswax and silicone polish.

Polish fills the porous surface of the timber and it builds up a protective layer on the surface of the material.

The polish can be applied...
- by hand with a cloth
- using a buffing wheel.

Polishing Metals

Metal polish is always slightly abrasive as it cuts away the surface of the metal until it's very smooth.

The polish can be applied with a buffing wheel. Polish can come in...
- liquid form
- a wax bar.

Polishing Plastics

The cut edges of hard plastics, e.g. acrylic, are often polished. Polishing can also be used to remove fine scratches. Polish can be applied...
- by hand with a cloth
- using a buffing wheel.

Compounds, e.g. Vonax, can be put on the buffing wheel and this allows a high gloss surface to be achieved. But, if you press too hard the edge of the plastic can overheat and this can permanently damage the plastic's surface.

A Buffing Wheel

Glazing Ceramics

Fired clay is **glazed** in order to seal and/or decorate the surface.

Glazed Candle Stick

There are lots of different glazes and results can vary greatly. Clay (which contains alumina and silica to make glass) is mixed with a flux (to help with melting) and other chemicals to add colour, textures, opacity (cloudiness) and feel.

Woodash glaze	Oatmeal glaze	Silky white glaze	Shiny glaze
Produces colours from greenish-grey to honey-yellow.	Gives a waxy appearance on the surface.	A strong white glaze, especially good on porcelain.	Produces a glossy, glassy glaze.
Wood ash 40 parts Felspar 40 parts Ball clay 20 parts Firing range 1240–1260°C	Potash felspar 49 parts China clay 25 parts Dolomite 22 parts Whiting 4 parts Firing 1250°C	Felspar 50 parts Zinc oxide 22 parts Whiting 10 parts Tin oxide 8 parts Firing 1250°C	Lead bisilicate 75 parts Felspar 30 parts China clay 7 parts Whiting 5 parts Firing 1250°C

Glazing Food

Food products are glazed to improve their appearance, for example to provide a smooth shiny coating or to change the colour of a surface to a golden brown. For example…

- honey and orange mix is used to glaze ham
- milk is used to glaze breads and pastry as it aids browning
- beaten egg is used to glaze pastry
- sugar syrup is used to glaze cakes and buns immediately after cooking.

Enamelling

Some metals or metal products can be **enamelled**, e.g. copper and cookers.

1 A powdered glass mixture is evenly applied over the surface of the metal.

2 The mixture is heated to 1000°C and melts.

3 On cooling a hard decorative coating is formed on the metal.

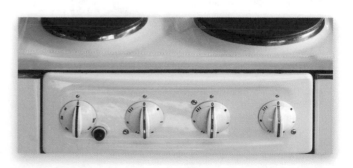

Printing

Lithography

Printing is a common finishing process used on a wide variety of materials.

Lithography is used mainly for commercial printing, e.g. paper and card. It can sometimes be used to print onto metal, e.g. soft drink cans.

The process works on the basis that oil and water don't mix:

1. Specially treated plates, normally made from aluminium sheet, are photographically exposed.
2. The unexposed parts of the plate (the image) attract grease (the ink) and reject water.
3. The exposed parts of the plate (the area not being printed) reject grease and attract water.

CMYK Colours

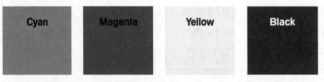

Cyan	Magenta	Yellow	Black

Lithography is usually **offset**, which means that the plates are made the correct way round (easier to check). They then print onto a plain roller that reverses the image before printing onto the paper. This is called **offset lithography**.

Some printing machines are only designed to print one or two colours. This is called **spot colour lithography** and is used for products like letterheads.

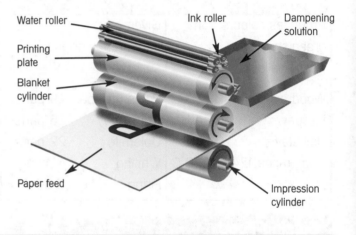

Labels: Water roller, Ink roller, Dampening solution, Printing plate, Blanket cylinder, Paper feed, Impression cylinder

Screen Printing

Screen printing is a simple process used to print onto a wide variety of materials including fabric, paper, plastic, timber and metal.

You can screen print in school:

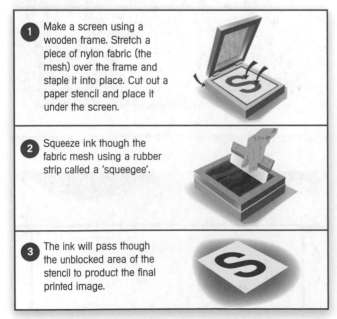

1. Make a screen using a wooden frame. Stretch a piece of nylon fabric (the mesh) over the frame and staple it into place. Cut out a paper stencil and place it under the screen.

2. Squeeze ink though the fabric mesh using a rubber strip called a 'squeegee'.

3. The ink will pass though the unblocked area of the stencil to product the final printed image.

Nylon is normally used for the mesh, but silk is the best material to use because it's very fine. This gives the term 'silk screen printing'.

The following process is used in industry:

1. Stencils are made using a photo-sensitive emulsion, which is applied to the screen.
2. The screen is then exposed to UV light using an acetate to mask off the desired shape of the design to be printed.
3. The UV light fixes the emulsion so the ink will not pass through it.
4. The parts that have been masked can be washed out of the screen so that ink can be forced through the mesh.

Screen printing can be done by hand or by using a variety of semi-automated machines. The printing machines and the cost of producing the screens is relatively cheap so the process is suitable for short print runs.

Flexography and Block Printing

Flexographic printing is used in industry to print onto plastic film or paper, e.g. plastic and paper carrier bags.

You can use this method of printing in school.
1. A raised layer of flexible rubber / plastic is attached to a roller.
2. The roller is inked and pressed onto the paper / plastic film.

Block printing is a very popular printing method used to print decorative fabrics. It's very easy to use in schools, e.g. potato prints, and you can use a variety of materials as the printing surface, e.g. Neoprene sheet:

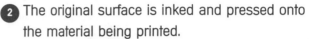

1. A block of material, e.g. wood or lino is cut into.
2. The original surface is inked and pressed onto the material being printed.

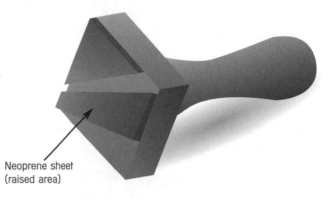

Neoprene sheet
(raised area)

Embossing

Embossing is a form of stamping where part of the surface is raised above the surrounding area. It's used…
- as a surface finish to paper or card
- to emphasise part of a design
- to suggest a quality product.

You can make simple embossing tools using either of the two methods shown.

Method 1

MDF

Polystryene sheet with design milled through

Paper

Neoprene sheet

MDF

Method 2

Shape to be embossed is cut with 1mm cutter. Piece that is removed is held onto adjoining board with double-sided tape

12mm MDF hinged together to allow even pressure when paper/ cardboard sheet is in place

N.B. This tool works by simply standing on it

Quick Test
1. How does a wax polish protect a piece of wood?
2. How does a metal polish work?
3. Why would you glaze a piece of fired clay?
4. What two materials is lithography usually used to print on?
5. Why is a card embossed?

KEY WORDS

Make sure you understand these words before moving on!
- Polishing
- Glazing
- Enamelling
- Printing
- Lithography
- Screen printing
- Flexographic printing
- Block printing,
- Embossing

Practice Questions

1 What is forming?

....

2 Explain when a batch production is used.

....

....

....

3 What does EPD stand for?

....

4 Which systems do manufacturers use to ensure that every item produced is of the same high quality? Tick the **two** correct options.

    A Quality dimensioning ◯

    B Quality assurance ◯

    C Quality control ◯

    D Quality inspection ◯

5 Name two metals that can be shaped by sand casting.

    a) ....

    b) ....

6 What type of product is made by slip casting? Tick the correct option.

    A Hollow, metal shapes ◯

    B Solid, rubber shapes ◯

    C Ceramic shapes ◯

    D Hollow, rubber shapes ◯

7 What kind of motion is used by jigsaw blades?

....

8 What does AFD stand for?

....

9 Name the two types of ceramic firing.

a) ....

b) ....

10 The table contains the names of six wood joining methods. Match descriptions **A**, **B**, **C**, **D**, **E** and **F** with the methods **1–6** in the table. Enter the appropriate number in the boxes provided.

	Wood Joints
1	Wood screws
2	Butt joint
3	Dovetail joint
4	Nails
5	Housing joint
6	Lap joint

A A corner joint for boxes, which is strong if glued ◯

B A joint used for holding up shelves in a cabinet ◯

C A weak fastening, which only relies on the strength of the glue ◯

D Permanent fastenings that can be removed with a screwdriver ◯

E A very strong joint, which can only be pulled apart in one direction and is used for drawer constructions ◯

F A temporary fastening that can be pulled out again after the glue has dried ◯

11 How is aluminium protected to make it durable and corrosion-resistant?

....

Answers

Design Development

Quick Test Answers

Page 7

1. **Accept any two of the following:** New materials; Iconic products; Manufacturing and technological developments; Fashion; Trends; The current thinking.
2. Industry
3. **Accept any suitable answer, e.g.** DeLonghi toaster; Chrysler cruiser
4. Designs often designed using computer technology characterised by a lack of straight lines.
5. **Accept any two suitable answers, e.g.** Coca Cola bottle; Biro; Volkswagen beetle

Page 11

1. Market pull and technological push.
2. To make the products more popular with consumers who know that certain standards have been met.
3. **Accept any three of the following:** Developments in new materials; Changes in manufacturing methods; New technologies; Social changes; Changing fashions
4. **Accept any two suitable answers, e.g.** Development of new materials; Introduction of electricity; Development in technology; Social change of women going out to work, etc

Answers to Practice Questions

Pages 12–13

1. a)–b) **Accept any two of the following:** The discovery of new materials; Iconic products; Manufacturing and technological developments; Fashions; Trends; The latest thinking
2. D
3. C
4. straight; CAD; flowing
5. D
6. Beetle; shape
7. B and C
8. **Accept any suitable answer, e.g:** BS EN ISO 9000:2005; Kitemark
9. Groups of workers who feedback information to ensure that the quality of a product is always improving.
10. Consumers see a product that they like and they start to buy it. This leads to development of the product and new, more advanced versions.
11. A 3; B 4; C 2; D 1

Design Issues

Quick Test Answers

Page 17

1. Meeting the needs of today without harming / damaging the planet for future generations.
2. That a fee has been paid to recover the packaging.
3. **Accept any two suitable answers, e.g.** Clothing; Shoes; Car parts; Plastic containers; Milk or drink bottles
4. The amount of carbon produced by any human activity.
5. **In any order:** Protection; Information; Display; Transportation; Containing; Preservation

Page 20

1. Using graphics / pictures
2.
3.

4. A design that meets the needs of everybody.
5. Because it focuses on small groups and caters a design to their particular needs / requirements.

Page 24

1. 5th–95th percentile = 90%
2. Work triangle
3. Anthropometrics
4. People living and working together.

Page 27

1. By manufacturing groups and by Acts of Parliament.
2. A test against nationally recognised standards.
3. The promises that a company makes to its customers.
4. Intellectual property.
5. A minimum price for the farmer and a premium to invest in development projects.

Answers to Practice Questions

Pages 28-29

1. A
2. B, C and D
3. a) A percentage of recycled materials have been used in production of the packaging.
   b) Product can't be disposed of in normal household waste.
4. B
5. Products that have been deliberately designed to have a very short life and will be disposed of soon after manufacture.
6. a) Fragile, handle with care.
   b) Do not allow contents to get wet.
7. C
8. a) how people work and live together
   b) how the brain works
   c) physical limitations of people
9. It's the study of efficiency of people in their working environment.
10. D

Materials

Quick Test Answers

Page 34

1. Cellulose fibres
2. By heating tiny chips of wood with water and chemicals together.
3. Board
4. **Accept any suitable answer, e.g.** Fast food lid containers
5. **Accept any two of the following:** Grain pattern; Colour; Texture; Workability; Structural strength

Page 39

1. Ferrous metals contain iron, are magnetic and can become rusty. Non-ferrous metals don't contain iron, aren't magnetic and don't rust.
2. Thermosetting plastics are not affected by heat. Thermoplastics are re-formed by heat.
3. **Accept any two of the following:** Melamine formaldehyde; Epoxy resin; Polyester resin; Phenol formaldehyde; Urea formaldehyde

4. **Accept any two of the following:** HDPE; LDPE; Polypropylene; Nylon; PVC; Acrylic; PET

Page 44

1. By firing at a high temperature.
2. **Accept any two of the following:** Cotton; Wool; Silk; Linen
3. **Accept any two of the following:** Polyamide; Tactel; Polyester; Acrylic; Elastane; Aramid
4. As glass reinforced polyester (GRP).

Answers

Page 47
1. Starches (cereals, bread and potatoes)
2. Body growth and repair
3. Fruit and vegetables, and carbohydrates
4. It stops a mixture from separating into its component parts.

Page 49
1. **Accept any one of the following:** Cheap to buy; Easy to assemble; Easy to maintain; Consistency of products
2. **Accept any one of the following:** Have to rely on supplier; Specialised parts can be in short supply; Need to monitor quality of suppliers
3. Input, process, output and feedback
4. Rotary, linear, reciprocating and oscillating

Page 53
1. **Accept** camera flash or flashing lights
2. Ohms
3. The number of teeth that it has.

4. A lever is a rigid bar that pivots round a fixed point (fulcrum).
5. Small reciprocating movements

Page 55
1. It turns into solid metal.
2. Changes in heat.
3. **Accept any one of the following:** Luminous signage; Luminous novelty toys
4. It will shrink by up to 5%

Answers to Practice Questions
Pages 56-57
1. B
2. B
3. **a)–b) Accept any two of the following:** Straight-grained but knotty; Cream /pale brown in colour; Fairly strong but easy to work with; Cheaper than a hardwood
4. contains iron; is a mixture of different elements
5. C

6. A and C
7. A
8. B
9. weight; volume; grams; litres
10. D
11. It's often the style of components that marks the different designs, e.g. having distinctive hinges unique to a single designer
12. The pendulum of a clock swinging from side to side in an arc.
13. Volts
14. Farads
15. B and D
16. They are woven into a fabric sheet and then impregnated with an epoxy or plastic resin and forced into a mould.

Processing Materials

Quick Test Answers
Page 59
1. To turn raw materials into useful stock sizes.
2. Conditioning
3. **Accept any suitable answer, e.g.:** Furniture; Bread
4. Mass production, probably 24/7 continuous

Page 62
1. Computer aided manufacture
2. Everyone working on a project can access the same information and be kept up-to-date with any changes /amendments.
3. Quality assurance
4. **Accept any two of the following:** Dimensional accuracy; Taste; Material quality; Electrical safety; Flammability

Page 67
1. **Accept any two of the following:** Cast iron; Aluminium; Brass.
2. Ceramics
3. **Accept any suitable answer, e.g.** Ball or plastic wheel.
4. **Accept any suitable answer, e.g.** Hats
5. It moulds heated plastic onto the shape of the former and the softened plastic is held by the vacuum until it's cooled.

Page 71
1. Plastics, e.g. PVC, Polystyrene
2. Folding bars and bending machines.
3. The grain of the metal hasn't been interrupted.
4. A cutting or slicing action such as that of scissors.
5. At least 3

Page 73
1. Cold chisel
2. Firmer chisel, bevel-edged chisel, mortise chisel and gouge.
3. Horizontal paring, vertical paring and chopping.
4. A clean, flat-bottomed hole.
5. Cutting large diameters in thin materials.

Pages 75
1. Up and down
2. Cutting and engraving materials
3. A tailstock is used to hold one end of the wood to steady it and is used when drilling holes.
4. **Accept any three of the following:** Roughing tool; Knife tool; Round nosed tool; Parting tool; Boring tool
5. **Accept any three of the following:** Skew chisels, gouges, scrapers and parting tools

Page 77
1. The grading shows how fine or coarse the paper is – the lower the number, the coarser the paper.
2. Timber and hard plastics
3. Conduction
4. Radiation

Page 79
1. Between -1°C and -8°C.
2. The bacteria have all been killed so it won't go off.
3. To make it tougher and less brittle.
4. They permanently fuse together.
5. The fusing of metal powders at high temperature

Page 81
1. The dovetail joint
2. It has a larger surface area for gluing.
3. Dowels
4. They are used as temporary joints to hold things together while glue dries or in carpentry and general building work.
5. **Accept any one of the following:** Cabinet screws; Pronged nut; Cross dowel; Modesty block; Cam lock

Page 85
1. In welding, the metals being joined are melted, in soldering a bonding alloy is melted and used to join the metals.
2. Metal Inert Gas.
3. It's a cheap and safe rubber solution.
4. Solvent-based paint, e.g. Hammerite™.
5. Oil-based paint.

Page 87
1. The oil will protect the timber from the wind and rain.
2. Wood stain doesn't protect the timber from moisture.
3. Thermoplastic, e.g. polythene and nylon.
4. Dip it in a bath of molten zinc.

Page 91
1. The polish fills the timber's porous surface and builds up a protective layer.
2. It works by abrading the surface of the metal until it's smooth.
3. To seal the surface and decorate it.
4. Paper and card.
5. To raise the surface and make it look more expensive / higher quality.

Index

Processing Materials (Cont.)

Answers to Practice Questions
Pages 92-93

1. Changing the size and shape of a material without altering the volume.
2. It is used to make a series of identical products that are made together in either small or large quantities.
3. Electronic Product Definition
4. B and C
5. **a)–b) Accept any two of the following:** Cast iron; Aluminum; Brass
6. C
7. Reciprocating motion
8. Accelerated freeze dried
9. **a)–b)** Biscuit firing and glaze firing
10. A 6; B 5; C 2; D 1; E 3; F 4
11. Anodising

Index

Acknowledgements

P.4 ©iStockphoto.com/Stan Rohrer/ Juergen Bosse/Mark Evans/Ian Hamilton
P.6 ©iStockphoto.com/Eric Wong/ Achim Prill/Hugo Chang
P.8 ©iStockphoto.com/Juan Monino
P.15 ©iStockphoto.com/Jonathan Scheele/Dar Yang Yan/Scott Savage/Michael Brown
P.19 BSI Product Services www.kitemark.com
P.20 ©iStockphoto.com/Terry J Alcorn
P.22 ©iStockphoto.com/Dar Yang Yan
P.25 ©iStockphoto.com/Jeremy Edwards
P.26 ©iStockphoto.com/Oleg Prikhodko
P.27 ©iStockphoto.com/Zsolt Nyulaszi
P.31 ©iStockphoto.com/Annie Desaulniers/Natallia Yaumenenka/Alex Slobodkin/Kevin Thomas/ Diane Diederich
P.35 ©iStockphoto.com/Debi Bishop
P.38 ©iStockphoto.com/David Meharey

P.39 ©iStockphoto.com/Yuriy Panyukov
P.41 © Linda Wilson
P.41 ©iStockphoto.com/Robert Dant/ Valerie Loiseleux/Dave White
P.44 ©iStockphoto.com/Danila Krylov
P.46 ©iStockphoto.com/Elena Schweitzer
P.47 ©iStockphoto.com/Michael Valdez
P.54 © In the Studio Jewellery School
P.58 ©iStockphoto.com/Sergey Dubrovskiy
P.61 ©iStockphoto.com/Christian Lagereek
P.69 ©iStockphoto.com
P.74 ©iStockphoto.com/Andris Daugovich
P.76 ©iStockphoto.com/Owen Price
P.76 ©iStockphoto.com/Madeleine Openshaw
P.82 ©iStockphoto.com/Owen Price
P.83 ©iStockphoto.com
P.84 ©iStockphoto.com/Daniel R. Burch
P.88 ©iStockphoto.com/Achim Prill

The following images are reproduced with the kind permission of Sealey. www.sealey.co.uk
P.16 H1104827
P.31 H1103262
P.68 DF910
P.70 3S-4R.V2
P.71 SM43.V3
P.72 AK6093; CC19G

The following images are reproduced with the kind permission of Rapid Electronics Ltd., Severalls Lane, Colchester, Essex CO4 5JS. www.rapidonline.com
P.50 112680; 356057; 810142; 081500; 231900; 551770; 130657; 180256; 632379; 603240; 820192; 370140; 283090

All other images ©2009 Jupiterimages Corporation, and Lonsdale.